DATE DUE			

PIGEON FANCYING

PIGEON FANCYING

Caring, Breeding, Racing
and Exhibiting

Ron Bissett

DAVID & CHARLES
Newton Abbot   London   North Pomfret (Vt)

Photographs and drawings by Philip Lovel
except where otherwise stated

British Library Cataloguing in Publication Data
Bissett, Ron
  Pigeon fancying.
  1. Homing pigeons
  I. Title
  636.5'96 SF469

ISBN 0-7153-8427-9

Typeset by Photo-Graphics, Honiton, Devon
and printed in Great Britain by
Butler & Tanner Limited, Frome and London

for David & Charles (Publishers) Limited
Brunel House Newton Abbot Devon

Published in the United States of America
by David & Charles Inc
North Pomfret Vermont 05053 USA

Foreword

Pigeons are the only creatures you can keep which you can give their complete freedom and which, when released hundreds of miles from home, will still return to their loft. The thrill never fades of seeing an old favourite returning from a race which began in France at a point four or five hundred miles from home, after twelve or fourteen hours on the wing.

Indeed on the day of our longest race from Nevers in France, a distance of 520 miles from my loft, I hear, perhaps, that the birds have been released at 6.00am in a north-west wind; I think 'It is a head-wind, they will fly at about 35 mph, that is fourteen and a half hours for the 520 miles. They should be home at about 8.30pm this evening.' During the day I am calculating from time to time how far they will have come and how far they still have to fly. I listen to all the weather forecasts and the shipping forecasts. I probably telephone a friend on the South Coast to enquire about the visibility over the Channel.

Then, perhaps at about 6 o'clock in the evening, it starts to rain, but I go down to the garden to the loft to wait, thinking, 'Perhaps they may do forty miles an hour', and when finally at nearly 9 o'clock a pigeon comes over the trees to land on your loft at your house, having flown for fifteen hours to reach home, believe me it is a tremendous thrill which only a pigeon fancier can have the pleasure of experiencing.

I sometimes compare pigeon racing with horse racing. In horse racing you are either the breeder, the owner, the trainer, the punter or the jockey. In pigeon racing you are all of these except that there are no jockeys.

I am delighted to have been given the opportunity to write

the foreword to Ron Bissett's book. He has been a friend for many years and, having spent over fifty years in the sport, he is well qualified to write it. Many books have been written about pigeons, but most of them are many years old and this new book is therefore very welcome. I particularly welcome the Chapter entitled 'The International Scene' which sets out the conditions applicable to pigeons exhibited at the Olympiads.

Over the last fifteen years the International Fédération has been one of my particular interests. One of the objects is to foster friendship between fanciers of all nations. Those who have been to the Olympiads and mixed with the many thousands of fanciers attending from all over the world will know that the love of the racing pigeon is the common bond which holds us together and will have experienced the companionship and friendship which these gatherings afford.

The dove is the symbol of peace. The racing pigeon can fly from country to country and cross frontiers without passport and without hindrance as easily as we travel to the next town. May we in due time be able to do the same.

I wish this book every success.

Guy C. Barrett
President of the Fédération Colombophile Internationale

Contents

List of Illustrations

Introduction

It should perhaps be admitted that pigeon keeping is not particularly high on everybody's list of sports or pastimes, mainly because it is not, strictly speaking, a spectator sport, but in the majority of cases is practised from a fancier's own home. There is, however, something fascinating about pigeon keeping. I remember that, when I was a boy of about six, one old fancier, Albert Harford of Hornsey in London, said to me, 'It's a disease and if the bug ever bites you'll find it hard ever to break from it'. How true this has proved, for I have spent practically the whole of my life in the absorbing sport of pigeon racing and have made many friends during thousands of miles of travel throughout the world as a result. In fact, the slogan devised by *The Racing Pigeon*, a weekly newspaper published especially for pigeon-racing fanciers — 'Racing pigeons, a family hobby from childhood to retirement' — is true of my life. I first became a member of my local club at the age of eight and by the time this book is published retirement will be on the horizon.

The history of the use of pigeons is of great interest. Birds of the dove family have been used for message carrying for thousands of years. Everyone knows the story of Noah and the Ark, and how the dove returned with the leaf of a tree; while in the British Museum there is a bas-relief showing the use of doves for message carrying in ancient Egypt about 2600BC.

In Mesopotamia about 4500BC, terracotta figurines of pigeons were made; the goddess of love, Astarte, had the pigeon as her symbol, and they were used by the ancient Greeks to carry messages. The Romans domesticated pigeons for food, religion and message carrying; the *columbarium* was an impor-

The moment of release (*Simon McBride*)

tant building in most villas of the time and some held 5,000 birds. The Romans also enthused about good pigeons, and gave huge prices for good breeders. People have not changed much in 2,000 years!

In medieval times every monastery, abbey and manor had a dovecote in order to supply fresh meat, for in those days the wintering of farm animals was impossible except for the breeding stock. Therefore all surplus cattle, sheep and pigs were killed and salted in the autumn, and through the long winter months of monotonous salt-meat, fresh pigeon must have been a great delicacy. Not until Viscount Townshend introduced the turnip for winter feed in the early eighteenth century did this change.

The pigeons of the lord or abbot were strictly preserved: no villein could catch or kill one, no matter how often they raided his crops. How they must have been hated by the peasantry. The dovecotes grew larger and grander, so that from simple timber buildings they became enormous brick or stone constructions, usually square or circular, with a central exit for the birds at the apex of the roof. There were many small breeding cavities on the inner face of the walls — the original 'pigeon hole', ingenious ladders for reaching every nest and, at ground level, a door for human access both to collect the birds and also to dig out the manure. This was prized even more highly than the birds, for its richness made crops grow better than anything known to man at that time.

As messengers, pigeons became more and more important both for military and commercial use. Roman and Saracen generals used them; Reuter made his fortune by using them to transmit information on stock-market dealings; horse-racing results were carried to London by pigeons, and in the Franco-Prussian war of 1870 and World War I pigeons were constantly employed for communications.

During World War II their use was even more extensive, and besides the lofts set up by the services there were many voluntary lofts of the National Pigeon Service comprised of members of the racing pigeon organisations who bred and supplied pigeons free to the military authorities. This service was considered so important, particularly in saving aircrews ditched in the Channel, that the government allowed the virtual extermination of the pigeon's natural enemy, the peregrine falcon. Some thirty-two pigeons were awarded the Dickin Medal, an award given for heroic actions by animals and known as the animal VC.

Although fanciers had enjoyed their little flutters earlier, the organisation of pigeon racing as a sport really began with the forming of the National Homing Union in 1897 with its headquarters in Leeds, its first secretary being A. Selby Thomas. Later the headquarters was moved to Gloucester, and when Selby Thomas died he was succeeded in the post of secretary by his son Joseph, who remained in office for many years; he saw the organisation given its charter and become the Royal National Homing Union. He retired in 1968, having served the union for forty-four years, for thirty-five of which he was general secretary. Shortly after his successor, Major L. Lewis MBE, took over, the organisation received permission to change its name to the Royal Pigeon Racing Association and about the same time the headquarters moved to Cheltenham. This organisation, together with five Homing Unions, covers the United Kingdom.

Pigeon racing is a family sport and anyone of virtually any age can be involved. Only recently I visited a friend whose four-year-old grandson was confidently holding a pigeon in his hand and proudly pointing the bird towards parents and grandparents. At the other end of the spectrum, I was not long ago chatting to a gentleman aged sixty-six who had just been bitten by the pigeon-racing bug, was setting up his loft and keen for any advice that experts could give. It is also a truly democratic sport, in which people from all walks of life can compete on equal terms. In an ordinary club you can find highly successful businessmen with plenty of financial backing, a considerable amount of spare time and the means to employ paid help. But they are by no means always at the top; the man with the small back-garden loft and only a few birds

Beachcomber, one of the thirty-two racing pigeons awarded the Dickin Medal for gallantry in World War II (*Courtesy* The Racing Pigeon)

owner, so that they will be extra keen to return to the calm and peace of their home loft with its human companionship. This is where lady fanciers are usually successful, and the loft which has the co-operation of a fancier's wife and family seems generally to be out in front. Pigeon racing is a time-consuming hobby: another pair of hands undoubtedly helps at busy times. Also, leisure time, holidays and money are often sacrificed by the family to make the loft successful, and undoubtedly it helps if this aid is given voluntarily rather than grudgingly!

Like other sports, pigeon racing has an international significance in that fanciers from many nations meet in true friendship at the Pigeon Olympiad and Congress which is staged by the International Federation every two years. Nearer home, in 1983 the Royal Pigeon Racing Association had a membership of almost 133,000. Added to this, the membership of the Scottish Homing Union, the Welsh Homing Union, the Irish Homing Union, the North of England Homing Union and the North West Homing Union gave a total membership in the United Kingdom of around 250,000 racing-pigeon fanciers, keeping probably about 8 million birds. In addition there are many more who keep birds at their homes just for pleasure, or who keep the high-flying Tipplers and Rollers, or exhibition types such as the Fantail and the Norwich Copper. Chapter 14 is devoted to their interests.

Perhaps the fascination of pigeon racing was best brought home to me many years ago by a young fancier who had just left school and had his birds sited three or four miles from his home on allotment ground. He used to walk the three miles there and back in the morning to see to his birds before going off to work; he would walk the six miles again in the evening, such was his enthusiasm. When I asked him what there was for him at the end of all this patience and effort, he replied that it gave him a sense of creating something; as he put it:

We fanciers plan the breeding of our pigeons, we train them, we give them the best of our attention, we make them comfortable at

18

home and then when we see that small bundle of some sixteen ounces of a feathered friend come hurtling into home at the end of a long race the feeling is indescribable. It is not a sense of elation but a feeling of closeness to that bird which has been cultured and developed by us – one which we have helped to create and train.

Such were the thoughts of a young lad many years ago, and the feeling he described is one I have experienced many times. Even though I may know that the birds returning to my loft are some considerable time behind the winners, there is always that feeling of contentment that they are back home with me, and that sense of achievement even though they may prove to be last in the race. It is hoped that this book will lead others into the sport, as well as helping those already in it, so that they too can share feelings which I myself have enjoyed over a period of fifty or more years.

I
The Pigeon Loft

Before thinking about obtaining pigeons it is essential to purchase or build a suitable house or loft for them. It need not be anything gigantic or luxurious but it should be built remembering that not only is it the pigeons' home, but that you will need to spend a lot of time there with them; for one of the secrets of successful pigeon racing is to create in the birds a love of home and of their owner.

There are those, of course, who can afford to build something like pigeon palaces — large permanent constructions to accommodate considerable numbers. But such is the equality of our sport that neither the size of the home nor its surroundings guarantee great achievements. You cannot buy success in pigeon racing. Many years ago a fancier known to the author kept his birds in a basement area in Victoria Street in central London only a few minutes' walk from the Houses of Parliament, and those birds were racing very successfully into five large sugar boxes which their owner had obtained from a manufacturer who used such containers for transporting sugar all over the world. These boxes were only about 76cm (2ft 6in) square and 1m (3ft) deep but, turned on their sides with an entrance fitted to the open end, they made a perfect home for each of the five pairs of birds which were all he ever kept. These birds would dive in unerringly from a race over London's traffic each to its own box.

It may be wondered why the building for housing pigeons is called a 'loft'. This is probably because in earlier times in Britain most pigeons were kept in high buildings. One old fancier told me over fifty years ago that the reason for this was to keep the birds away from poachers, although he said that

Villa Patience, the aptly named lofts of Pierre Dordin who is seen here with his wife, dog and pigeons. Villa Patience is at Harnes near Lens, France

some of these clever fellows used to employ small boys to climb up through the small entrances to take the birds. In Belgium, pigeons' accommodation is still mostly found under the roof of the family home, in what is usually termed the 'loft' and normally used in Britain as storage space. Many leading Belgian fanciers have had their houses deliberately built to a design with enough loft room to ensure they have the housing they need for their pigeons.

So although most of the pigeon houses in Great Britain are now in gardens, the description of them as lofts is understandable. In some parts of Great Britain the loft is described by other names; for instance in the Midlands it is referred to as 'the pen', whilst in Northumberland and the Scottish Borders it is known as 'the cree'. Further north in Scotland it is the 'ducat', a colloquialism for 'doo cote'; for many north of the Border refer to their pigeons as 'doos'.

Ready-made lofts are available and are advertised quite regularly in the papers devoted to the sport. There is,

22

however, a great deal more fun in building your own pigeon house, if you have the ability. If you decide to build your own loft, there are a number of important points to bear in mind. One is the cost, for it is important that pigeons should be a hobby and not just a drain on one's pocket; you must build what you can afford. Secondly you must consider the number of birds you intend to keep, for it is wrong and dangerous to overcrowd them. You should allow about $0.6m^3$ (20cu ft) per bird.

Particularly if you live in a built-up area there may be local restrictions or council regulations, and you should always check details of these before building a pigeon loft. Most local authorities today permit them, but if there are problems the Royal Pigeon Racing Association through its regional officers, or the officers of the appropriate homing union, will take the matter up with the authority on behalf of members. This is one of the many advantages that membership of the association or unions offers at very modest membership fees.

The next point to consider is the siting of the loft. This, in built-up areas, will probably be controlled by the size of the

The magnificent lofts of Claude Hetru in Belgium

back garden, but the loft should be as far from other buildings as possible, with a view to obtaining maximum sun. Generally it is thought best to site it facing south or south-east, but if this is not possible adjustments in construction can be made. For instance, my first loft had to be sited facing west, so I arranged an opening on the southern side which allowed all possible sunshine to enter the loft throughout the day. During autumn and winter I covered the southern-end opening with a glass frame, thus shutting out the driving rain of the prevailing south-west wind.

If, because your garden is too small or because of local regulations, you cannot have a loft at your home, you may still be able to keep pigeons. Particularly in the north-east of England there are areas where fanciers have their lofts on allotments, and in parts of south Wales lofts are situated on the side of slag heaps. In some cases such devoted fanciers walk two or three miles to their lofts carrying fresh water at least twice a day.

If an existing out-building, garage or attic can be taken over, it will of course save much time and expense. Avoid anything that has contained poultry, for many diseases can be transmitted to pigeons, especially coccidiosis. Brick buildings have many advantages over wood, for they are inherently drier, less prone to condensation, warmer in winter and cooler in summer.

One other point in the placing of the loft must be the consideration of the position of other buildings in relation to the birds' drop-in. It is important that there should be as few obstacles as possible in the approach for, if a bird has to circle several times before making its landing, valuable time is lost in a race.

Fig 1 shows the plan of a very popular type of wooden structure which has been approved by many councils in Great Britain. When building your loft remember it should be completely dry and waterproof; for as much as sunshine is a friend to pigeons, so damp is an enemy — in damp lofts disease will quickly develop. You must also be careful to start

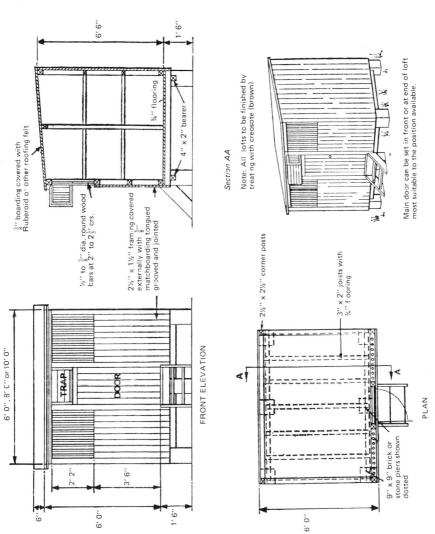

5/8" boarding covered with
Ruberoid or other roofing felt

6' 6"

1' 6"

3/4" flooring

4" x 2" bearer

1/2" to 5/8" dia. round wood
bars at 2" to 2 1/2" crs.

2 1/2" x 1 1/2" framing covered
externally with 5/8"
matchboarding tongued
grooved and jointed

Section AA

Note:- All lofts to be finished by
treating with creosote (brown)

Main door can be set in front or at end of loft
most suitable to the position available.

6' 0", 8' 0" or 10' 0"

TRAP

DOOR

FRONT ELEVATION

6"

2' 2"

6' 0"

3' 6"

1' 6"

2 1/2" x 2 1/2" corner posts

3" x 2" joists with
3/4" flooring

A

A

PLAN

6' 0"

9" x 9" brick or
stone piers shown
dotted

Fig 1a   Design for loft as approved and recommended by the Royal Pigeon Racing Association

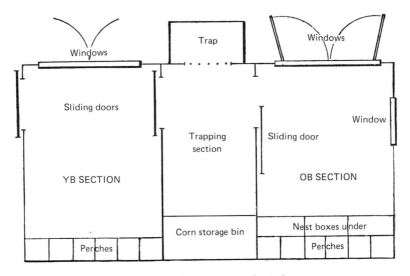

Fig 1b   Internal plan for loft

with a plan which will suit your own personal requirements, remembering that when you are in the loft you will need room to move around quietly, working among the birds and near enough to talk to them at the same time.

It is important to make sure you have a good strong floor — 1.5cm to 2.5cm (½in to 1in) thick boards supported by 5cm (2in) cross members on 7.5cm × 7.5cm (3in × 3in) runners the length of the loft. It must take more than your own weight, for at some time or other you are certain to have visitors with you. But, although strong, it should be portable. The floor of, for example, a 5.5m × 1.8m (18ft × 6ft) loft, could well be made of three sections 1.8m (6ft) square. Portability, in fact, applies to all parts of a loft. Construction should be in sections, and the sections should be joined only with nuts and bolts so that, if the loft needs to be moved, the job can be easily done.

It is not necessary to obtain all new materials for building the loft; some well-designed lofts have been built of timber obtained from packing cases. Generally the wood covering the sides should be approximately 1.5cm (½in) thick; the width of the planks does not really matter although it is desirable, for

26

appearance sake at least, to maintain uniformity of width on each side of the loft. The usual is wooden planks approximately 10–15cm (4–6in) wide, and if you can obtain these in tongue and groove this will help to ensure a close fit, thus assisting damp proofing.

The lower part of the front of the loft should be covered in up to a height of about 1m (3ft). The upper part should consist of dowel rods 1.5cm (½in) in diameter, set about 5cm (2in) apart. These may be covered with netting of 7mm (approx ¼in) mesh to keep out wild birds such as sparrows or starlings which will carry diseases to your birds, and eat their corn.

All horizontal surfaces will need to be scraped regularly to remove the pigeons' droppings; therefore it is very important that there are no joints in which dirt can lodge. Even tongue-and-groove boards are not ideal because in time the wood will shrink and leave gaps, or expand and rise up, causing splinters as you scrape it. Plastic vinyl tiles or hardboard have all been used to give a good scraping floor, which will save you hours of time in the long run.

Interior partitions are usually made of thin wooden laths nailed to 2.5cm or 4cm (1in or 1½in) quartering, screwed to the floor and walls of the loft. Partitions should be removable, in case you wish to alter anything. Each partition will need a door, and if possible these should be of sliding type to save space when opening them. In the normal 5.5m (18ft) × 2m (6ft) loft, two partitions provide three sections — one in which the breeding will be carried out and to which the old birds will race, one for any pigeons you do not intend to fly out (stock birds) and one into which the young birds will be transferred and to which they will race in their first season. During winter the sexes can then be parted into two of the three sections.

Ventilation

Ventilation is of great importance in the loft, fresh air being essential to the health of pigeons. The design of your loft should therefore provide a steady flow of fresh air but not

A typical garden loft: note the louvres for ventilation at floor level

draughts. As a start, the loft should be raised at least 23cm (9in) from the ground, preferably on brick pillars, to allow a steady flow of air beneath. It is as well to surround the support with small-mesh wire netting to prevent marauders such as cats, hiding under the loft waiting to pounce on any bird which may alight on the ground. Bury the lower edge in the ground and turn it outwards to discourage rats and mice from tunnelling under your loft, for the latter will eat the corn and rats will kill the pigeons.

Internal ventilation should provide air circulation in the form of inlets in the front provided by louvres about 30cm (12in) wide × 20cm (8in) deep set about 10cm (4in) above floor level, and an outlet opening about 10cm (4in) deep along the top of the back of the loft. This opening should be covered by narrow-gauge 'Twilweld' or wire mesh. The louvres should be set so as to give at least one in each section of the loft. Avoid draughts, for cold pigeons cannot give of their best, and never have ventilation which will let rain beat into the loft.

28

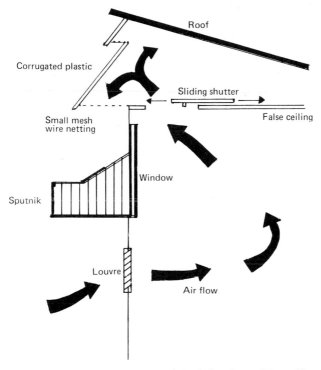

Fig 2 Controllable ventilation of the loft using a false ceiling

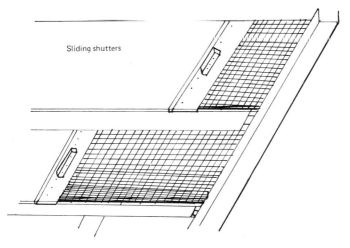

Fig 3 Adjustable shutters in the ceiling allow stale air to escape

29

Trapping Mechanisms

Trapping, or persuading the birds to enter the loft as quickly as possible after their return from a race, is probably the most vital consideration; and you may find, even after building your loft, that it becomes necessary to adjust your methods.

Many different types of trapping have been tried. In earlier days most fanciers adopted the piano-type with bob wires (Figs 4 and 5). One drawback with this method is that the bob wires have a tendency to slow a bird's entry into the trap; for a pigeon after flying 320 or 480km (200 or 300 miles) had to push the bob wires with its wing butts which, after a hard race, tend to be a bit sore. It is better to replace the bob wires with the drop-hole method, whereby the entrance to the loft is divided by the insertion of semi-circular pieces of wood at intervals, wide enough apart to allow a bird to drop into the trap, but narrow enough for it to be unable to get out again, as it cannot stretch its wings to fly out. There is another form of this on the market called the Anti-bolt, made out of galvanised wire (Fig 6). A similar principle is used in the Belgian Sputnik. If these are set along the full length of the loft

Two Sputnik traps: on the right the birds can come and go freely — an 'open' loft

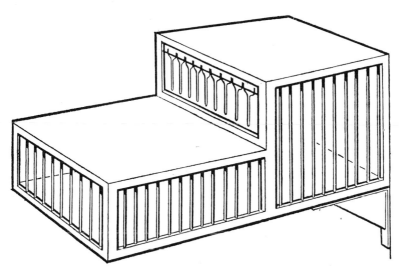

Fig 4　The piano-type trap

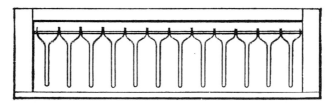

Fig 5　Bob wires as set in the trap entrance

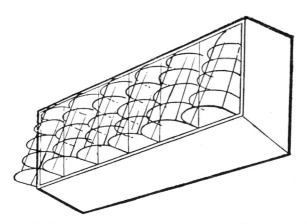

Fig 6　Anti-bolt wires set in trap entrance, as seen from inside the loft

All pigeons love a bath, especially young birds. Make sure that surplus water can run off so that the whole loft does not become drenched

Birds enjoying sunshine in a Sputnik trap

entrance and a let-board — sometimes known as a pitch-board or landing-board — on which the birds drop is set at about eye-level, by raising your hand to the let-board you can control the bird's entry into the loft. A bird will then go direct to its own nest-box or perch, and be quietly waiting to be picked up if it is to be clocked in.

Another advantage with this method is that a wire cage (like a small aviary), the length of the let-board and the depth of the drop-holes, can be placed in position over the let-board. The Anti-bolt sections, hung on their metal hooks, can then be removed, leaving the opening free so that the birds can fly up into the wire frame and sit on the let-board in the sun. This is particularly useful with young birds, which can be placed in the frame to enjoy the sunshine and re-enter the loft when they wish, without fear of their being frightened by anything going on around them. In this way they learn a good deal about their surroundings before attempting to fly.

Perches

Perches within the loft act as a pigeon's own private place of rest, and in most lofts each bird will take its own particular perch. Always be on the lookout, when young birds are weaned, for those which have claimed the uppermost perches; these generally turn out to be some of the most courageous racers. It should be quite possible in a well-managed loft to go in after dark and pick up any particular bird.

Perches are of many types but the three I have used most are the box perch, the triangular, saddle or V-type perch and the pedestal perch. The first, as its name implies, means that each bird is provided with a box of its own about 30cm × 30cm (12in × 12in) by about 15–23cm (6–9in) deep. Thus a construction 1.2m (4ft) square would provide sixteen box perches. They are best made from planks of wood whose width is the same as the chosen depth of the perch — my favourite is 15cm (6in), but many prefer the greater depth of 23cm (9in) because the birds are more easily caught in them. Generally the wood is 13mm (½in) thick.

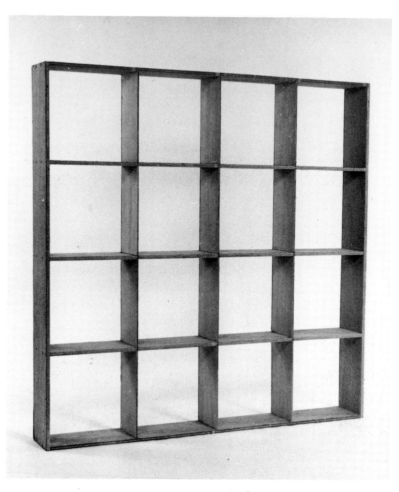

Box perches

The triangular, saddle or V-type perch is made by taking two pieces of wood 15cm (6in) square, shaped off at one end at an angle of 45°. These two pieces are fitted together over a length of wood 13mm (½in) square, a small piece of plywood or hardboard is attached and the whole thing is then screwed to the wall through the plywood or hardboard.

The pedestal perch is not generally used except by fanciers who are interested in the showing or exhibition side of the sport. It is, as the name implies, an individual perch, and

The saddle or V-type perch (*Shepherds Basket Works*)

Loft interior showing use of saddle perches (*Rick Osman*)

consists of a circle of wood 3in in diameter on top of a piece of 4cm (1½in) dowelling or quartering about 6in high fastened to a square base screwed to the floor of the loft. Such perches can be set in various places on the floor, one for every bird in the loft. They are useful for show enthusiasts because they overcome the risk of any droppings hitting and staining the tail or flights of another bird. The same advantage applies to saddle perches if they are staggered against the loft wall, but box perches come below one another.

Nest-boxes

Nest-boxes (Fig 7) provide pigeons with places for their private lives, and after your birds are mated or, as some fanciers prefer to say, 'paired', they will spend a considerable time in them. They should therefore be of a size which two birds and two youngsters can share comfortably — about 60cm (2ft) × 60cm × 60cm. It is useful to have a shelf the full width of the box and about 25cm (10in) from back to front, set about half-way up the box. In this way two nest-bowls (see Fig 7) can be accommodated as required during the breeding season, and when one bird is sitting the shelf provides a perch for its partner and gives an extra sense of calmness to the birds. It also allows the hen to retreat if the cock is too aggressive. The thickness of wood for nest-boxes is usually 1.5cm (½in), but this is a matter of individual taste.

The positioning of nest-boxes depends on your individual loft. In general they are placed along the back of one of its sections but, if your loft has to be narrow from back to front, nest-boxes can be made triangular-shaped to fit into a corner.

Opinions differ considerably among fanciers concerning the entrance to nest-boxes. Some prefer the opening to be the complete top half of the removable front, let down on hinges to form a let-board or perch the full length of the box. Fanciers who prefer this say it provides somewhere where the pair of birds can rest together when not nesting. Others prefer the opening to be 15–18cm (6–7 in), square allowing only one

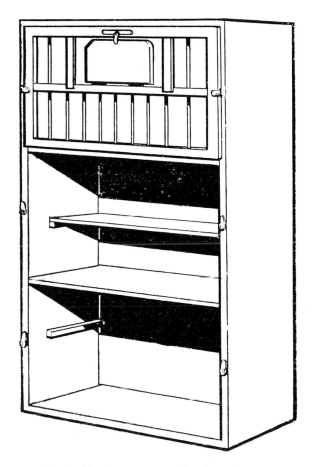

Fig 7   Nest boxes as used by the author

bird to enter at a time. This opening may be in the upper half, or at floor level which has the advantage of letting an intruder get out quickly when attacked by the rightful owners. If he cannot see the exit, all three adults will mill round and round, destroying eggs or young in the process. Yet others, equally successful, do not believe in putting in fronts at all, and never seem to have any trouble with the mating of birds or fighting because birds enter strange nest-boxes. This is just a small example of how different the methods of pigeon fanciers can be.

A cock sitting contentedly on eggs. Note the door at floor level for easy exit; the nest box front is set back to form a perch and the sliding door cannot close accidentally

The same box with door closed. Note record card for entering details of the date of laying and hatching and the ring numbers of the youngsters

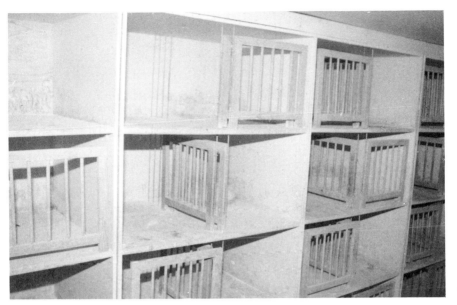

Another type of nest box front. These wooden doors turn on metal rods, and can be fastened into different positions according to the fancier's wishes

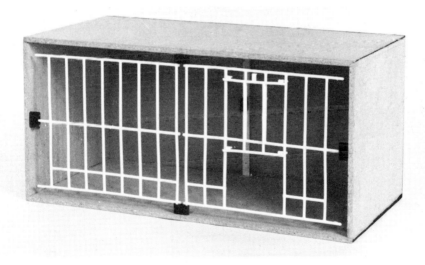

A widowhood nest box. By arranging the two doors in different positions, the fancier can: a) confine the cock and the hen together in the whole nest box; b) confine the hen in one half, allowing the cock to return to the other half on race days; c) have the hen on eggs in one half and the two squeakers in the other; d) close the box completely outside the breeding and racing seasons (*Shepherds Basket Works*)

Nest-boxes can be arranged in tiers of three or four according to the height of the loft, but make sure they are not higher than you can reach. Preferably have the entrance to the top box of the tier at eye-level, because if you have to make an effort to reach into a nest-box or perch the pigeon will sense this strain and will not be confident of your approach; and you must always have the confidence of your birds. To save money, tea-chests can be used as nest-boxes and burned after one season's use. Those from China are best, for they are of solid wood, not ply, and they lack the sharp metal strips which can cut human fingers and birds' toes.

Miscellaneous Items

There are a few more necessary items, one of the most important being the water-fountain or trough. A regular supply of clean water is essential; pigeons can go quite a long time without food, but not without water.

The water-fountain consists of a round plastic or galvanised bowl over which a cone with vertical bars is placed; the birds are able to drink from the bowl between the bars, but the cone shape prevents the water becoming contaminated. The trough, as its name implies, is open along the top; and arrangements should be made so that birds cannot sit on the sides of it.

Whether you use a drinking-fountain or a trough depends on the design of your loft. If you have decided on wire netting for the loft front or have covered over the dowels, it will not be possible to use one trough for internal and external drinking, although an arrangement can be made for inside the loft, putting the drinking-trough on a shelf surrounded by a frame with vertical wooden bars, so that birds drink between these bars. I prefer to have one trough for both inside and outside use. On the outside it should be covered with a piece of thick-gauge clear plastic material hinged to the loft, to give access for filling, allow light through for the birds to see the water and protect against marauding felines.

A water bowl with removable lid for feeding and filling. A loft with pigeons will easily drink four to five pints of water daily, especially in hot weather or when they are feeding young birds

A drinking trough for use either on a basket or on the exterior of a loft (*Shepherds Basket Works*)

Another essential item is a grit-hopper — a regular supply of fresh grit being very important to pigeons. There are several on the market, but a handyman can soon make one for himself very cheaply. The same ease of construction applies to the feeding-trough or hopper. Some fanciers feed direct on to the loft floor, but however clean you keep this there is always danger of the corn being contaminated by excreta. I have

41

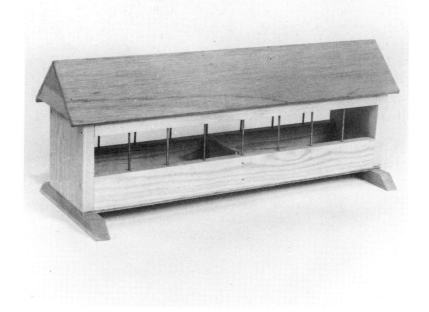

A wooden feeding trough (*Shepherds Basket Works*)

always used a food-hopper based on the design of the drinking-fountain but oblong in shape, about 60cm (2ft) long by about 15cm (6in) wide with a tray approximately 9cm (3½in) deep, and with openings above through which the birds can reach the corn. The depth of the tray stops the birds from spilling corn over the floor.

Nest-bowls are another requisite. They are usually about 20cm (8in) in diameter and 9cm (3½in) deep. Those available on the market are usually earthenware, and these are the most popular with fanciers. In recent years, however, a much cheaper type has become available, made of compressed paper-pulp and disposable after use. When nest-bowls are placed in nest-boxes, it is advisable to half fill the bowl with coarse clean sawdust to cushion the eggs. Lastly, at breeding time some short cuts of straw or tobacco stalk can be placed in a convenient place in the loft. The birds will enjoy carrying these to their nest.

This, then, is the outline of the requirements of your loft. Remember, as was said earlier, that the loft should be designed to the needs of the birds but also for your comfort and pleasure, making work within the loft as simple as possible. A well-built pigeon loft, properly maintained, can last many years; in fact there are fanciers still racing to the originals they erected forty or fifty years ago.

2
Obtaining Your Pigeons

With your loft erected, it is time to think of obtaining your initial stock, either to act as founders of your family of pigeons or as birds to race. If you have not already approached your local club, now is the time to do so. If you know a local fancier, contact him for the address of the club secretary; if this is not possible, the regional secretary (see Appendix I) will supply you with addresses of clubs in your area.

Once you have the address, telephone the secretary who will probably be only too pleased to help and who will advise you of the best way to start. Since you are still feeling your way, he will probably advise you to join the club as an honorary member; usually this will involve quite a small sum, say around £1, and will save you paying an entrance fee to the club until you are really ready. Being an honorary member will allow you attend the club meetings and activities and will provide for your immediate need, which is to meet and talk to practical fanciers who are usually willing to assist newcomers in any way they can. Although as an honorary member you will not be able to take part in the business side of the club, you will gain insight into the administration and general running of the sport. The president or secretary will probably personally introduce you to the club's leading or champion members. Generally, each locality has its own outstanding or star fanciers; some may be owners of large lofts and possibly widely known, others are regularly successful in their own area with just a small team of birds and quite a small loft.

In talking to these local successful fanciers you will begin to understand the necessity for keeping records in order to plan the breeding and management of your pigeons; for most will have built up their families of birds by a constant policy of eliminating any weaklings and of making sure that their breeding programme is directed towards obtaining success and maintaining quality.

Many fanciers, after their ruthless selection of their teams each autumn, find they still have a few birds which are surplus to the accommodation available in their lofts. These are regularly advertised in *The Racing Pigeon* and *British Homing World* at quite reasonable prices. Also every year during the non-racing season there are a series of auctions at which detailed breeding information — generally described as pedigrees — of the birds on offer is often available. When reading these the newcomer to the sport should be very careful, for high-sounding names are often given to strains of racing pigeons which have been bred over the years from many generations of unraced or untested stock, the names being maintained simply because many generations ago one bird owned by a particular fancier put up an outstanding performance. It is always possible that another successful racer may be

A pigeon auction sale. Potential buyers examine each lot minutely before the bidding starts

purchased under these conditions, but we are now talking of the newcomer purchasing stock on which to try to build future success. So once again the advice is to seek out and meet a local fancier who has been winning consistently as the best source of your very first birds.

The old saying, 'you have to learn to walk before you can run', is very true in pigeon fancying, and the friendship of a successful local fancier can be the guiding hand whilst you are learning to walk. In addition, obtaining your stock from successful local fanciers ensures that the birds you start with are acclimatised to the local environment. Do not spend too much at first on buying the very best; you will make many mistakes in the first few years, and it is better to learn with cheap birds than very expensive ones. When you have perfected your own methods of management and training, then is the time to buy the very best that you can afford. By then you may also have decided whether to specialise in sprint, middle- or long-distance races, and your choice of which strain to buy will in part be governed by your preference.

This is not to belittle those fanciers of national and international repute who regularly put up good performances in national races, and who concentrate primarily on just that. If you want to obtain birds from such fanciers, they often advertise in the pigeon-fancying press with details of these successful winning families, and they usually provide birds of high quality. Most fanciers with a recognised name in the sport can be relied on, and would never think of offering birds for sale which do not measure up to their own standards. Generally, the birds they offer in autumn and winter are, as already mentioned, surplus to their requirements due to lack of accommodation or they are birds bred that year. These young birds, of course, have all their life before them. They may have taken part in two or three races but have not been over-strained and could be future champions.

Broadly speaking, there are three ways to obtain birds:

An aviary for stock birds. The wire-mesh floor keeps the pigeons from contact with their droppings

1 To purchase pigeons and breed from them in your own loft. This includes old pigeons and those hatched the same year.
2 To purchase young birds early in the season, say in March, April or May to train yourself.
3 To obtain eggs from the fancier of your choice as well as some ordinary birds to hatch and rear the youngsters. Remember if you do this that 'feeders' have to be bought and mated before purchasing the eggs from the fancier.

If you decide to adopt the first course and want to obtain birds which have succeeded in races and have flown long distances or won outstanding positions, do not be misled into thinking that you need birds of considerable age. Birds of two, three or four years may prove quite a solid buy, but birds of extreme age will probably be worn out or on the downgrade and would not be a worthwhile purchase, especially to the newcomer to the sport.

Personally, if I were starting again, I would adopt this first method; but the birds I would buy would be yearlings — those born in the previous year and which have completed one season's moulting. These would mate reasonably quickly, and after two or three months of breeding you could reasonably reckon to 'break' or settle them to your own loft (see p 66). Thus, providing you make your birds comfortable and happy in their new home — and nothing could be more conducive to calmness and happiness than raising their young in the quiet presence of their owner — you should be able to get them to fly from and back to their new home. However, there is always the risk of losing them and, if they have cost a lot of money, it may be essential to keep them as prisoners.

I would not advise a newcomer to go out and purchase late-breds with a view to breeding from them, particularly if he is keen to race young birds in his first season. For these late-bred birds — that is those hatched out of season, say in July, August or September — although usually less expensive, need time to mature before one uses them to breed.

This raises another important point which must be stressed — namely personal patience. Do not think you can rush things when trying to settle birds to your new loft. If purchasing yearlings, as suggested above, it is best to do so about the end of January and let them occupy one of the three sections of the loft for a couple of weeks or so before you mate them, or pair them, about mid-February. Let them quietly rear their first nest of youngsters without going out; then, whilst they are sitting the second pair of eggs, you can attempt to settle them as described below.

Patience is even more necessary if you decide, because of financial limitations, to buy your initial stock as late-breds. In this case you must be prepared to allow considerably longer for the birds to settle to their surroundings and to mature. It would, in fact, be advisable to purchase these birds in September or October of the year they are born; in this way you might be able to settle them to your loft and have them flying out before you consider mating them.

If you decide you want to follow the second course, my advice would be to purchase, say, six or eight young birds of about four weeks old. These will soon get used to their section of the loft and, although there will still be that anxious time which all fanciers go through annually — that of settling young birds — if they are given a good chance to see the outside of the loft and obtain a fair view of the immediate surroundings before they become too strong on the wing, the risk of loss will be considerably reduced.

As described earlier, if you have a wire cage to cover the let-board, you can put this in place and remove the drop-holes so that young birds can go through the opening into the cage, where they can enjoy the sunshine and develop a knowledge of their surroundings. They can also become accustomed to any sudden movements and noises while nevertheless being shielded from them. After a few days, on a good but not too bright a day, remove the wire cage from the let-board before removing the Anti-bolts and retire a short distance from the loft to watch your birds. When the youngsters come out they will begin to flutter their wings, and in a few more days will be going up into the air and back to the loft.

You may have decided on the third method and purchased birds to use as feeders and obtained eggs from a successful fancier. When the eggs have hatched and the young birds have been reared successfully, the latter can be removed from the parent birds to the section of the loft earmarked for young birds, and the settling programme begun as for young birds bred from yearlings or older birds.

In settling yearlings after you have bred the first nest of youngsters, as previously mentioned, the wire frame again plays its part because, when they are not sitting, the birds can spend the time in the frame having a look around. When first allowing the yearlings freedom outside the loft, the best method is to place a bowl of water on the let-board so that the pigeons can take a bath. They really do enjoy this and,

49

especially on a warm sunny day, will bathe and then lie in the sun preening themselves. Because their feathers are wet they will not be so strong on the wing, and will therefore be less likely to take off and lose themselves before they have a good 'fix' on home. When I moved to a new loft some thirty years ago, I had four cocks and four hens to settle. During the time the birds were rearing the first nest of young birds, I placed the bath inside the loft. Then, when the young birds were about three weeks old, almost ready to wean, and the old birds had just started sitting again, one Sunday I placed the bath on a table a very short distance away from the let-board and retired inside the house to watch from a window. Very shortly the four cocks were out of the loft, into and out of the bath and lying sunning themselves on the let-board. One after another, as the time came for them to take their turn on the nest, they went back into the loft without any trouble. Soon afterwards the hens were enjoying themselves in the bath, then spent some time on the loft and two of them even took a flight around the loft; but at the end of the day all the birds were comfortable and happy in their nest-boxes. From then onwards they were let out daily and only one strayed back to the old loft, just for one day.

But, of course, everything comes easier if the bird is of good quality to start with. How can the newcomer judge the right bird whichever method he chooses to follow when starting? To some extent he must be guided by the fancier or fanciers he goes to in order to obtain his pigeons. It must be remembered that few fanciers have lofts full of champions, also that champion racing birds are not all champion breeders. If purchasing older birds, seek out fanciers who, according to their birds' pedigrees and records, have shown themselves to breed pigeons to perform consistently. In buying yearlings, select birds which have shown a tendency to race consistently, even if not actually winning, as young birds. In other words, choose birds which have regularly been among the early ones back to the loft.

Selection of young birds really falls into two categories. If

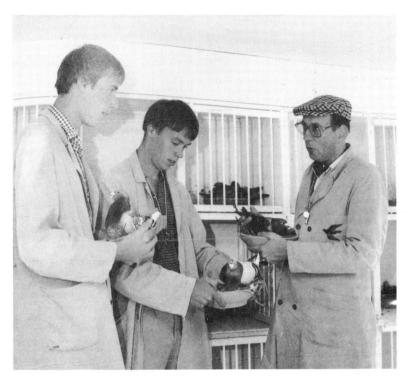

Constant selection: Hans Eijerkamp and his two sons with three of their best breeding cocks

you intend to race the youngsters you purchase, they should come from proven breeders. But if you intend to keep the youngsters as your own breeding stock, they should come from birds that have raced successfully; for although the best racing birds do not necessarily produce good racers direct, the next generation is once more successful.

There are, of course, exceptions to this generalisation and you will meet fanciers anxious to quote these exceptions. In addition, there are today several reputable breeders who are specialist stockmen particularly interested in breeding so that other fanciers can race their stock. Through the expertise of these fanciers, the blood lines of many champions have been blended in a way that was not known some thirty or forty years ago. These breeding birds are often housed in large stud farms which enjoy national or international reputation.

To sum up, before you finally make up your mind to purchase, study the advertisements in the papers devoted to the sport and the very popular Year Books published by them; talk to local fanciers in your area about what you read and about their own history of breeding and racing. Never be afraid to seek advice from others, for this is a sport in which one never ceases to learn.

3
Life-cycle of the Pigeon

Sex Differences and Courtship

Having considered the preparation of accommodation for your birds and the obtaining of stock, let us turn our attention to certain facets of the life-cycle of the pigeon itself. One of the first problems for a beginner is how to determine the sex of his birds. This is something which will come with practice, though fanciers who have been in the sport for many years can still make a mistake.

Firstly it must be realised that, as in most birds, there are no visible sex organs; also that, unlike other types of birds, there is no characteristic difference in colour between the sexes. Differences of colour are the product of inheritance. However, a fancier gets to know his family of birds individually, and usually, if he is an owner of some years' standing, can sort out their sexes. He may have difficulty though in dealing with pigeons to which he is unaccustomed.

There are one or two general guides which may help. For instance, the cock is usually larger than the hen and this is noticeable from the day of hatching. Also, as a rule, the cock bird has a bolder looking head with the crown higher above eye-level; the hen's head has a less-pronounced crown and the eye therefore appears to be set higher. Besides this, the hen's general appearance seems altogether more sweet and attractive, whilst the cock has a more aggressive look, although you will often hear older fanciers referring to a 'cocky looking hen' or a 'henny looking cock'.

Another guide is the preliminary action of courting, when you will see a cock bird apparently blowing out his crop and turning round in front of the hen bird whose attention he wants to attract. Although fanciers describe the enlarging of the crop as 'blowing the crop', it is not the crop itself which fills with air, but the air sac which lies over it. The hen will often coo and inflate her neck a little, but she will very seldom if ever spin round in a circle.

It is during courtship in the mating season that one obtains the best guide to the sexes. One should remember though that such behavioural differences are not confined to the actual mating or breeding season; even when birds are parted in different sections of the loft (see p26) you will see them displaying to one another through the partitions if they can see through them. In the case of hens, they walk slowly and somewhat seductively to lead the cocks on. The latter move more quickly with a fast movement rather like strutting, and bob their heads up and down whilst turning a complete circle. As courtship progresses, it leads to a further stage of 'beaking' — or 'billing' as some fanciers call it — when the hen puts her beak inside the cock's. They then ring beaks with an action similar to that made when they are regurgitating food to feed their young.

When the female pigeon is aroused, she will quite often follow the cock around the loft as if she were inviting a beaking session; or if the cock is still and resting, she will make a sort of stroking action down the back of his neck. This leads to the final stage in the birds' mating procedure known as 'treading'. Here the hen crouches down, opens her wings a little and the cock jumps on to her back, whereupon, by means of a slight movement to one side by the hen, copulation takes place. This action is very quick. Other cocks will, if possible, rush to prevent copulation, and may be successful if the cock is inexperienced or old. Some fanciers let out their breeding pairs one at a time so that successful mating is accomplished.

It is not unknown for two birds of the same sex to pair together, and you will find that if you have two hens mated they will both lay. Pigeons lay their eggs in clutches of two so that from the mating of two hens you will get four eggs, but they will not be fertile.

From Egg to Weaning

Normally the first of the two eggs laid appears about ten days after pairing and at 4.00–5.00pm. There may be the odd exception to this rule, but only on rare occasions have I heard of hens laying their first egg in the morning. The other egg is laid approximately 42 hours later — a little before noon on the second day after the first egg is laid. Incubation is about eighteen days from the laying of the second egg. Sitting on the eggs is shared by both sexes with the hen taking the largest part; normally she will sit from 4.00 or 5.00pm throughout the night until about 10.00–11.00am in the morning, when the cock bird will take over. While the latter is on the nest, the hen will have her exercise, and for this reason most fanciers try to coax their hens outside around this time in the morning. If a fancier has to go to work this can present problems, but usually there is someone in the family who will release the hens for exercise.

When the eggs have hatched, both male and female birds take their turn in feeding. During the period of sitting on the eggs, a cream-like substance commonly known as 'pigeon milk' forms in and adheres to the wall of the crop of both parent birds. Composed mainly of protein and fat, this soft food feeds the youngsters for the first three or four days. Newly hatched birds are devoid of feathers, but are covered with a small amount of yellow down. They grow quickly, doubling their size at about 5 days old, and they soon begin to grow their feathers.

It is during this time that a young bird's identity ring should be placed on its leg — when it is 7–8 days old. Some strains have much bigger feet than others, and so need ringing a day or two earlier. Check the next day that the ring has stayed on the leg, for it is a tragedy if a good young bird loses its ring as this will prevent it ever being raced. The ring is quite easily slipped round the three toes and pushed along the leg towards the body over the back claw which, being rather like a piece of soft gristle, can be eased out from the ring with no harm to the bird. This ring will now be on the bird's leg for life, because a

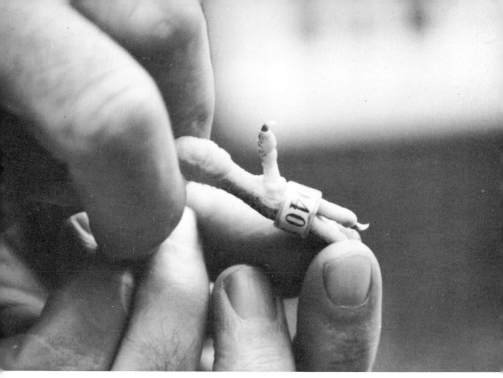

Ringing a seven-day-old youngster. The three front toes are bunched together

The ring passes over the ball of the foot

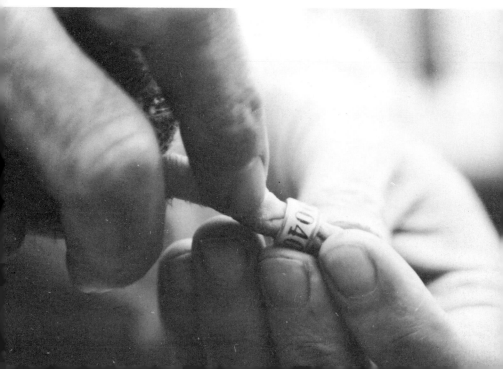

The ring slides up the leg and over the back toe, which is then pulled through the ring

The ring in place; it should be checked after twenty-four hours in case it has fallen off

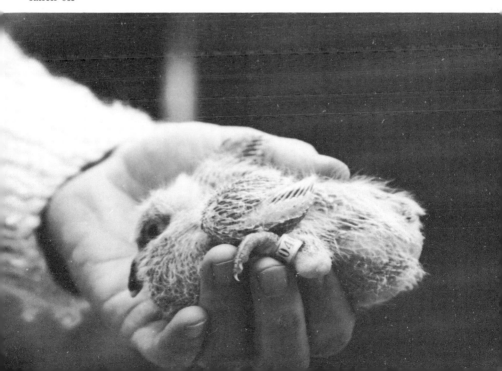

few days later it will not be possible to remove it without extensive damage to the bird's foot.

Around the sixth or seventh day, the young birds start to take different food, again with both parent birds taking part in the feeding. The latter fill their crops with corn, and after a short while regurgitate that food and literally pump it into the young birds. At about 14 days old the young birds will be almost fully feathered, and from around the age of 20 or 21 days you will see them beginning to move around in the nest-box and find them chasing the older birds in the hope of food. Shortly after this you may even see them, if there is corn available, picking up the grain for themselves.

Between the age of 24–28 days, the young birds are ready to be weaned from their parents. In some cases this weaning process can be adopted considerably earlier. I have been able to wean birds at 18–21 days old because they were forward in trying to pick up corn for themselves and were thus ready to be taken into the weaning pen to progress to the next stage in their development.

The earlier weaning can be done the better it is for your old birds, because the pumping of food into their youngsters requires a great deal of energy and can drain them considerably. For this reason young birds should not be allowed to stay with their parents after about 26 days. Early weaning also protects the youngsters from attack by older birds: cocks in particular will badly injure or even kill a young bird that strays into the wrong nest-box. In addition, young birds make better progress if they can be weaned quite early. On the other hand, do not rush things at this point. Just keep your eyes open so that you notice exactly when the young birds are attempting to feed from the pots of food which you have in the nest-boxes. The progress of the youngsters after they have been taken away from their parents is dealt with in Chapter 6 on Training, for young birds need to be trained from the moment they leave the nest.

When the young birds are approximately 14–16 days old, the hen will normally lay the first egg of her second clutch and this is again followed at the 42-hour interval by the second egg. Some fanciers prefer to replace these eggs with chalk, china or plastic ones on which the birds will sit in the normal way. This is an obvious advantage because the old birds will not be subjected to the strain of rearing the young birds hatched from this second round of eggs, and will therefore be reserving and building up their strength for racing later in the year. We cannot expect pigeons to be continually rearing youngsters and racing at the same time. The eggs can be discarded, or passed to 'feeder' pigeons to hatch and rear.

Naturally, if they are stock birds, they can be allowed to sit and rear the second clutch. Some birds will try to take over a second nest-box for this purpose, so watch out for fighting at this time.

Feathers and Moulting

We will first look at the pigeon's wing, for of course it is with the wings that the pigeon is going to do its flying and its racing. I remember over forty years ago listening to a talk of great interest given by the late John Kilpatrick, a knowledge-able and successful pigeon fancier from Belfast, and the way he described the structure of the pigeon's wing has always remained in my mind. The bones, as he put it, consist of the humerus or upper arm, the radius and ulna which correspond to the forearm; and the outer edge of the wing which is like the hand and fingers.

If you fan a pigeon's wing to its fullest extent, you will find ten longer pointed feathers towards the outside of the wing known as the primaries, and ten shorter feathers with more rounded edges situated nearer the body known as the secon-daries. The latter grow from the forearm, whilst the primaries are attached to what John Kilpatrick called the hand and fingers — six attached to the hand and four to the fingers. These four can be used independently, and in a very hard fly such as a race it is these four outside feathers which have to

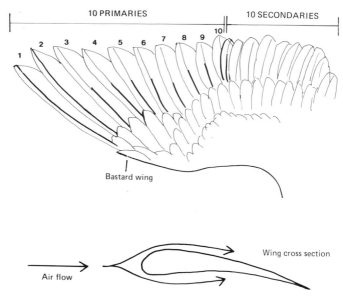

Fig 8   The wing of a pigeon in plan and cross-section

take the strain. I have often seen pigeons that have returned from a race with the quills of the outside four feathers bent considerably in towards the body, and with one even bent under its neighbour.

During the season, pigeons will go through a moult in which they gradually shed their feathers and grow new ones. This follows a very orderly fashion, and birds basically maintain their complete wing in that until one new feather is about three-quarters grown, the next feather will not drop. Formerly, fanciers used to regard the moult as being something of a disease so that the birds had to be really mollycoddled. This is not so; it is natural for a pigeon to moult, although during it one should keep an eye on the bird to make sure that shedding is progressing in order; that is, the secondaries and primaries are being shed starting from the part of the wing nearest to the body. If any bird appears to be a little off colour, take it away from the others and give it extra care and attention. Especially when a bird is moulting its last

60

two primary feathers (the two farthest from the body), do not force it to exercise or race. Particularly in young birds the growing of these two outside flights seems to be a somewhat taxing process.

The feathers are made of protein, just like muscle, and it is therefore essential that during the moult some good quality protein is included in the diet. This normally comes from the legume family: beans, peas and tares. At the same time carbohydrate is required to provide the energy needed for racing. If food is in too short supply when the feathers are growing, especially in young birds, a line of fretmarks will appear in the quill of each primary and secondary feather, and often in a stressful race the feathers will bend or snap at this weak point.

The tail of the pigeon contains twelve feathers and these are moulted two by two, in an orderly fashion. The first two to drop together will be those immediately either side of the centre two tail feathers or the fifth in from the outside on both sides. When replacements for these two are about three-quarters grown, the centre two tail feathers drop. These will grow again, and when they are about three-quarters long, the third set — the two feathers two places away from the centre two, or fourth in from each outer side — will fall. These will be followed by those three places away from the tail centre and also from the extreme outside; then the first feathers in from the outside will come away, and finally the outside two. This orderly moulting ensures that there are no big gaps for the air to rush through whilst the bird is in flight. Sometimes, however, young birds will drop two sets of tail feathers together, and rather ominous large gaps will appear. One important point to note is that during the period of moult, particularly when the smaller body feathers are growing, the birds should not be handled too much.

But although birds should not be handled unnecessarily, remember at all times that it is observation of your pigeons, the watching of each individual, that will give you the information which will lead to success in racing. Pigeon keeping is a 365 days a year hobby. Your birds need your attention at some time every day of every year.

The Homing Faculty

Many times the question has been asked, 'How do pigeons find their way home — what is the secret of the homing instinct?' It seems more appropriate to call it a faculty because it is something which can be developed. For instance, birds can be moved from one loft location to another, settled in and then raced successfully to their new home.

The homing ability of racing pigeons has been the basis of discussion and experiment over the years, but most fanciers seem agreed that when the birds are released they orientate themselves by the sun, then set off in the correct direction for their home lofts. One theory put forward was that birds pick up reaction from the earth's magnetic field and home along this; but this was discounted in an experiment by Dr G.V.T. Matthews of Cambridge about twenty years ago. He mounted very small but powerful magnets on the wing butts of pigeons, the magnets being arranged so that they totally disturbed the magnetic field. But although the birds took considerably longer, they still homed.

Fog and heavy cloud will slow birds down on their route, this giving added weight to the theory that they orientate by the sun. Yet surprisingly, the best flying days seem to be when there is broken blue sky and a slight wind; on very clear sunny days with the air still and with high temperatures, the birds seem to find the going really tough. On such days young birds are very easily lost from the loft itself. Electric storms also have an effect on the homing of pigeons. In fact some birds delayed by such a storm have been known to be absent from their loft for as long as six to twelve months.

In other words, the question of how pigeons find their way home remains a puzzle. If anyone ever finds the answer, the whole face of the sport could be changed.

4
Management of the Loft

Methods of management within the loft vary greatly between fanciers simply because keeping pigeons is an individual hobby to be enjoyed. Never let it become boring, or feel that it is just another job that has to be done. However, in all matters concerning breeding and general management of your birds there should be careful planning, one of the most important requirements being regularity and consistency of action. As far as is humanly possible, everything in connection with loft management should be regular, smooth, quiet and unobtrusive. In other words, the birds should be pleased to have you among them, and should know your routine as well as you know it yourself. Like most animals, they are creatures of habit. Find a system that suits you, your family, your work and the birds; then stick to it unless convinced that a change would be beneficial.

Breeding and Mating

Many happy hours can be spent in the dark winter evenings with plans for your matings the following year. Nothing must be left to chance, everything for and against a particular coupling must be considered. The whole affair can be like a jigsaw puzzle — you may not fit the right pieces together at the first attempt. Some fanciers pair their birds on paper hundreds of times before they find what they consider is the ideal mating.

That great fancier, Dr W.E. Barker, wrote in his very popular book *Pigeon Racing*: 'Luck and chance have no part in the scheme of creation; there is no law in nature more certain than the law of heredity.' These words of wisdom have always been uppermost in my mind when thinking of mating and their message that, although the breeding of racing pigeons may be a little less certain than that of other birds, it must be meticulously planned. Some fanciers, particularly those who have a thorough knowledge of genetics, plan their matings as much as two or three years ahead to make sure that things go as they would like them to. But for every fancier, a study of his previous breedings will show which family of birds has a tendency to be breeders and which successful racers.

Many things need to be taken into account when selecting birds for mating, but try to pair those which are physically suitable. Do not use extremely different types. For example, you will not necessarily achieve success by pairing a very large bird with a very small bird in the hope that you are going to strike a happy medium. It would take many years even for an advanced geneticist to be sure of doing that. Nor is the mating of very long birds to very short-breasted birds to be encouraged. The continual mating of birds which have a tendency to be oversized should also be avoided, as should the mating of extra-small ones. And one must keep one's eyes open to make sure that body size does not deteriorate, which often happens where fanciers practise too frequent and too close inbreeding. However, having said all this, you will always find exceptions to the rules.

It has already been said that every bird in your loft should be an individual to you, so never let the number of birds rise beyond your capabilities of management; keep the numbers small enough to note each bird separately. There has been a tendency in recent years for fanciers to breed larger and larger teams of young birds, and many of them are failing to make the grade and win prizes because of this reliance on numbers rather than on individual quality and individual attention. Only by careful observation and study will you learn the characteristics of the birds in your loft, and when you see these traits, don't rely on memory; write them down, including in your notes any faults you find. It is this learning in detail about each bird that makes pigeon fancying so fascinating.

Having studied your birds and decided on the actual couples you would like to see together, it is necessary actually to mate the pairs. The nest-boxes must now be the pigeons' homes, and it is preferable to allow the male birds to become accustomed to their nest-boxes first and well before the time of mating (see Chapter 15). With this in mind, I allow the cocks to occupy the nesting section of the loft during the winter period when the sexes are parted (see pp 68 and 69) and, as I never keep more birds than I have nest accommodation for, there are no perches in this section of the loft at that time. Each cock bird therefore soon sorts out for himself one of the nest-boxes, and will protect it against any other bird who may try to take it from him.

When the cocks have settled to their boxes — and if you adopt the method outlined above they will have had a considerable time to do so — each hen should be introduced to its particular nest-box in a quiet manner. The fancier must now watch quietly in the loft to observe whether the couples appear to be taking to each other. Such observation is essential to make sure the hens do not suffer from over-attention on the part of the cock. There is not usually much problem in this respect, but some cocks are so boisterous or even vicious that unless you take steps to stop their over-exuberance, which can approach pugnacity, the hen can suffer severe damage around the head or to the eyes. If the problem does occur, it is usually when an older cock bird which has been mated for several seasons to a particular hen is introduced to a new partner; it can also happen with over-excitable yearling birds mated for the first time. It is then best to remove the hen bird, or alternatively to place a transparent partition in the nest-box so that the birds can see each other but not make direct contact. Usually after a short period they will settle with each other quite well. Sometimes a block of wood or two bricks are needed in the nest-box to give the hen a refuge from the cock's attack. Even if the hen is quite amorous, some cocks will regard a new hen as an intruder to be ejected forthwith; having defended the box all winter it takes them some days to tolerate the presence of a mate.

The next step is to encourage the hen to become accustomed to the position of her nest-box in the loft. To achieve this it is advisable to open one nest-box at a time and allow a pair of birds out into the loft for just a few minutes. You will usually find that the cock bird, after a very short period, will fly back to his nest-box and the hen will follow at his call. During the next few days you will find that you will be able to open two or three boxes together, possibly one in each tier of boxes. If you use the type of nest-box illustrated on p 37, you can help prevent birds entering the wrong one by staggering the position of the nesting-bowls in the boxes, having them alternately on the upper and lower sections and on different sides. Once the birds have settled down on their first eggs, you should have no problems.

When the eggs are laid, generally around ten days from the pairing date, and the birds begin the incubation period, do not disturb them unnecessarily but let them carry on their sitting in as quiet an atmosphere as possible. You will be able to obtain a peep at the eggs when the birds leave the nest to feed, or when they change over on the nest, and feel all the satisfaction which comes from a mating successfully completed.

Culling

One must be almost ruthless in the selection of birds for mating. Any birds that for any reason seem doubtful or unsuitable should find no place in the breeding plans for your loft if you hope to succeed.

For me the perfect racing pigeon should be well balanced, without a tendency to tip forward if you hold it in one hand. It should sit snugly in your two hands and should have a good supply of body feather. The tips of its flight feathers (the primaries) should be 2.5–4cm (1–1½in) from the extreme of the tail feathers. The head or rather the skull-bones in the head, should be bold and well formed, indicating plenty of room for the pigeon's brain. The eyes should be well set in the head, clear and bright. I do not like very deep-keeled pigeons, those whose breastbone is at too great a depth from the backbone, so that the bird seems square at the front. The keel should be fairly long in comparison to body length; it should not finish abruptly, but should run straight with a gentle sweep upwards towards its finish just before the tail. On the other hand, avoid equally those birds which are too shallow with extreme lack of depth. This indicates lack of chest space and is usually a sign of poor breeding.

Day-to-day Routine

One important point in loft management is cleanliness. The loft floor should be clean and dry at all times, and the majority of fanciers scrape out any droppings daily and sprinkle coarse sand on the floor, or brush dehydrated lime powder into the wood. Others adopt the deep-litter system, putting down a layer of about 10cm (4in) of straw on the floor, so that the droppings go into the straw and dry up. The straw should be raked or turned about once a week, and changed about every four to five months. All drinking vessels should be thoroughly cleaned when water is changed; this should be at least once a day, and preferably more than once if you have time.

During the breeding season, droppings will accumulate around the outside of the nesting-bowls. They should not be allowed to become excessive, but a little accumulation around the bowl can provide extra warmth for the growing youngsters. The nesting materials (see p 42) within the bowls should be changed with each pair of eggs laid. If you adopt the type of nest-box recommended, a clean nesting-bowl with clean material should be placed in the nest-box on the shelf, or on the lower part of the box if the one in use is on the shelf, when the young birds are about fourteen days old. This will give the hen time to settle to the new nest before laying the next pair of eggs. In clearing around the nest in use, any eggshells or any eggs which may not have hatched should be removed.

The front of the nest box removed for easy cleaning

When the breeding and mating season has been completed, pairs should be separated to allow the birds to complete the moult in a peaceful atmosphere. The cock birds, both old and young birds bred that year, should be kept in the old-bird section of the loft where the nest-boxes are, and the hens can then be kept in the section which has been occupied by the young birds during the season. The nest-boxes should be thoroughly cleaned out and the removable fronts taken away, thus providing space for the cocks to sleep at night as they begin to select their boxes for the next season. After the birds are parted, the moult will proceed more quickly and care should be taken to clean out all cast feathers from the odd corners of the loft where they blow as the birds fly to and from their perches. If left, the feathers harbour disease and parasites, and the hens will gather them into odd corners and start to lay again.

Inbreeding, Line-breeding and Out-crossing

Inbreeding is the term used to describe the pairing together of close relations. Father × daughter, son × mother, or brother × sister, are all examples of close inbreeding. Line-breeding is really the same, but using relationships that are more distant, such as two cousins or two grandchildren paired together, grandfather × granddaughter or uncle × niece. The object is to intensify and fix in a family of pigeons the good qualities of a common ancestor; the disadvantage is that inbreeding or line-breeding will also tend to intensify any bad characteristics which may exist in the strain.

Therefore if you use this method — and very many fanciers do — it is even more essential to ruthlessly monitor events to make sure that the good features you want are still there, and that no bad ones are creeping in. Appearance and colour count for nothing; it is performance that counts. Even when inbreeding or line-breeding has been successful, there comes a point when a fancier may feel that it is time to bring in new blood. Perhaps, for instance, he detects that the birds are becoming smaller, particularly the hens; or he feels that his results in really tough races with strong headwinds are no longer so good. In that case he will search for another strain or family which excels in the size of its hens, or in its performance in rough weather. It is best not to buy in a bird just because its own individual performance is good; it must come from a consistently reliable winning family of pigeons.

Ideally these pigeons should also have been inbred or line-bred for some generations, for the crossing of two different inbred strains of any animal or plant often produces a phenomenon called hybrid vigour, whereby the progeny markedly outshine their parents. This has been noted many times in the pigeon world, where the introduction of new blood markedly energises an old strain. For example, the Cattrysse brothers in Belgium had an excellent strain that had raced well for twenty-five years; but when they introduced a Bostyn, and later a Stichelbaut, out-cross, the results were

The wing of a successful blue cock of the Cattrysse strain

spectacular even by their high standards. Some strains have become particular favourites for out-crosses because they seem to blend or 'mix' particularly well. The Stichelbauts just mentioned are one example; another is the Janssen strain cultivated by four brothers in Arendonk, Belgium.

However, other fanciers deliberately do not inbreed. They keep their pairings quite unrelated, and often buy many pigeons from different sources to make a complete mixture of bloodlines. And they can be equally successful. The late George Busschaert, for instance, was without equal in the buying and pairing of birds from many sources, and his successes were spectacular.

To sum up, there is no hard and fast rule; each fancier makes his own decisions on how to breed, rear the offspring and test them in the basket on race days. In the end, performance is the finest pedigree; and when you find that the birds bred from one particular mating regularly beat the opposition, rejoice greatly and never part or sell those two parents. You have perhaps struck upon the most elusive and sought-after prize in pigeon racing — a so-called 'Golden Pair'.

5
The Art of Feeding

There are many successful fanciers who claim that when you have mastered the art of feeding racing pigeons you are on the way to success, assuming of course that you have the basic successful bloodlines in your family. The late W.T. Carr of Tottenham, a mentor of the author, once said that there was no way that any feeding or management would make a bad pigeon into a champion, but by good feeding a mediocre bird could be improved and a good bird could be turned into a champion. But he also emphasised that feeding, like everything connected with pigeons, was something individual to both the fancier and his birds.

Like most birds, the pigeon has no teeth with which to chew the food it is given, so it has another method of dealing with what it eats — the grain consumed is stored in the crop, where it is moistened or softened, until it starts going through the digestive process. It then passes on to the stomach, which in the pigeon is quite small and cannot contain a large amount of food for any length of time. From the stomach the food moves into the gizzard, which has an outer covering of strong muscular-type walls and a very sturdy lining. It is here that the grain, with the help of grit which the bird will have taken, goes through the mill and is ground down and mixes with the digestive juices through which it has already passed on its way to the gizzard. From the gizzard the masticated food passes to the intestines, where it meets further secreted digestive juices and where the contents of the food are broken down further to enable it to be absorbed into the bloodstream.

Having briefly looked at how a bird consumes its food, we must consider what a healthy bird needs and what foods will satisfy those needs. Basically, they come under four headings: protein, fats, carbohydrates and mineral salts plus vitamins. Each is required for building up and maintaining the active functions of the pigeon's body. Protein is needed to build up body, bone and feather, and to replace worn tissues from time to time. Carbohydrates are the main sources of heat and energy, for although protein can also supply these it should not be regarded as satisfactory for the purpose, as an overloading of protein has a detrimental effect on the birds. This is because the bird breaks down the protein into carbohydrates and into ammonia which has to be excreted by the kidneys. The amount the latter can handle is limited, so that toxic ammonia and urate accumulate in the bird. So it really is a question of finding the correct balance. In general, a protein content of 17–18 per cent is considered correct.

To help the reader determine the value of the food he feeds to his pigeons, the following list takes an average of four sets of analysts' figures as to the contents of various grains and seeds:

	Protein %	Carbohydrates %	Fats %	Fibre %	Minerals %	Water %
Lentils	27.5	51.1	2.1	3.4	2.7	14.0
Tares	25.5	48.4	1.6	5.4	2.9	13.6
Beans	24.5	49.4	1.3	6.9	3.4	14.0
Linseed	24.3	22.0	37.4	5.5	3.8	7.0
Peas (maple)	22.0	44.5	1.5	4.6	2.6	14.0
Rape	19.0	18.6	45.0	5.9	4.2	7.3
Hemp	18.0	21.0	32.3	15.3	4.2	9.0
Canary seed	14.2	56.0	5.2	8.8	3.4	12.4
Wheat	13.2	69.5	1.9	1.9	1.7	14.2
Oats	11.2	60.1	5.4	6.3	3.0	14.1
Millet	10.8	64.3	3.7	8.1	1.8	12.2
Maize	10.5	67.1	5.7	2.2	1.5	13.5
Barley	9.5	68.7	1.9	4.5	2.3	14.9
Dari	9.0	70.4	2.4	1.9	1.4	12.5
Rice	5.8	80.5	0.5	1.5	0.6	12.3

These figures are a good guide for preparing your own feed mixtures. For instance, in order to provide the required protein content in a mixture, the formula would be to multiply the protein content of each type of grain used by the quantity of the individual grain in the mixture, add the totals together and then divide by the total quantity of the mixture. For example, take 4.5kg (10lb) of mixture comprising 2.7kg (6lb) of maple peas and 1.8kg (4lb) of beans; this would give:

Maple peas   protein content 22.0 × 2.7 = 59 (22.0 × 6 = 132)
Beans   protein content 24.5 × 1.8 = 44 (24.5 × 4 = 98)
                              Total 103   (Total 230)

Divided by 4.5 (10) this gives a protein content of 23%.

A 4.5kg (10lb) mixture of 1.8kg (4lb) of peas, 0·9kg (2lb) of beans, 0·9kg (2lb) of maize and 0·9kg (2lb) of dari would provide:

Peas   Protein content 22.0 × 1.8 = 40   (4 × 22   = 88)
Beans   Protein content 24.5 × .9 = 22   (2 × 24.5 = 49)
Maize   Protein content 10.5 × .9 = 9   (2 × 10.5 = 21)
Dari   Protein content 9.0 × .9 = 8   (2 × 9   = 18)

                          Total   79   (Total   176)

Divided by 4.5 (10) makes a protein content of 17.6%.

Any seed can be substituted for any other and the content worked out accordingly. The table can, of course, also be used to obtain the carbohydrate or other factor content of the feed which you are preparing for your birds.

We now know the usefulness of the various grain feeds to our birds, but how much to feed? On average, a pigeon will consume 25–40g (1–1½oz) of corn per day, varying slightly with the size of the bird. A larger pigeon may need more food to keep its body going, just as a more powerful motor-car engine will use more fuel per mile. A larger pigeon has more bulk and more weight to shift and therefore uses up more energy in its efforts, and this energy must be replaced if the bird is to be kept in reasonable condition or form. The daily food should be given approximately one-third as an early morning feed, and the remainder in late afternoon or early evening after exercise.

This brings us to the question of whether one should simply give more food, or whether it is better to study the content of the mixture you are feeding and prepare separate feeds for individual birds. A friend of mine, the late H.J. Humphrey of Tottenham who was very successful in racing, when preparing for longer distance races, mixed the corn and seeds for each particular pair of birds. For example, knowing that some birds would make flesh more quickly than others, he made sure he reduced the protein content for those particular birds, such was his meticulous fanciership.

There are many successful fanciers who do feed their pigeons in pairs or singly so that the birds obtain the right proportion of protein and carbohydrates that their owners have learned, by experience, they require. With young birds it is best to feed them by hand. This does not mean picking up each bird and putting the seeds in its beak individually, but to construct a feeding-tray, the size of which will depend on the number of birds you will be feeding. For feeding twenty-four young birds, the tray needs to be about 60cm (2ft) long × 30cm (1ft) wide.

The tray can be constructed by obtaining a piece of wood the size you require and fixing pieces of 50mm × 13mm (2in × ½in) battening upright around the edges to prevent the birds from throwing the corn over the floor when eating. With young birds do not pour all the corn into the tray at once, but only about half the quantity you intend to feed. In this way you can gradually add the rest of the food and at the same time talk to your birds and give them an occasional gentle stroke along the back whilst they are eating. This helps to make the birds confident, and to cement the link between you and your pigeons which is so essential to success.

With regard to old birds, the ideal is to feed each pair in its own nest-box, using the small troughs available on the market which can be hung on the box front. In this way the birds are fed quietly and without disturbance, particularly when they are nesting. The birds can reach the corn and eat it between the dowel or slatted front, and you can control the food for individual pairs. You can even, if required, vary the content of the food from pair to pair in order to bring the birds into the physical condition desirable for racing. All this comes with experience, but attention to feeding is one sure road to success.

However, the method described takes a great deal of time, and it is not possible for the average pigeon fancier who has to work all day. In a case like this, unless you have the help of a friend or wife, the birds have to be fed all together, and the best method of feeding is probably by food-hopper. Many fanciers adopt this way of feeding and say that if food is before them all day, old birds will only eat what they require; they will not overeat. There could be a lot of sense in this, and it is for the fancier himself to devise and follow the method which best suits both himself and his birds. Do not let the job become drudgery, otherwise you will find that you will neglect the small things and your powers of observation within the loft may decline. If you follow this method it is a good idea to give each type of grain in separate containers; if it is all mixed up the birds will waste a lot of it searching for the grains they prefer. Remember that whatever time you spend in the loft, for whatever purpose, is a time of contact with your birds. You should be observing them the whole time, and making notes of any little idiosyncrasies.

As regards the corn itself, one of the most important things is that it should be bought dry and kept so. Corn which has been subjected to dampness or sweating may become affected by fungoid growth and this can have a very bad effect on a pigeon's health. Storage is also an important factor, and corn should be stored in a cool dry place with, if possible, air circulating around it. Avoid metal containers such as dustbins, because there could be sweating, and thus deterioration. One of the best ways I have seen corn kept was in the lofts of the late Major W.H. Osman which were situated at the top of a building in central London. The containers consisted of boat-shaped wooden frames covered with a fine wire gauze and suspended by chains from the rafters; thus air could circulate around them at all times. In addition the corn was turned regularly with a scoop. However corn is stored, it should be turned over fairly regularly; but the main essential is that it should be kept dry and free from attack by mice, rats and wild birds all of which can transmit diseases to the corn and so to your birds.

On the subject of turning corn, two very successful fanciers known to the author would tip the corn received from their suppliers out on to a tarpaulin sheet on their lawn and turn it in the sunshine for two or three days, pulling the tarpaulin sheet over it at night to make sure it did not become damp. After the two or three days' turning in the sun, the corn was then transferred to their storage bins. This little anecdote again shows the importance of attention to detail.

Besides corn, birds need minerals in their diet. There are some excellent proprietary mineral salts on sale, but be sure also to give the birds mineral-rich green food regularly. One of the best green foods is watercress which is quite cheap during the summer months. But one of the best all the year round sources is cabbage, chopped quite finely and then dusted with a fine coating of ordinary table salt. The birds should have this twice a week; once they discover that it is salted they will eat it readily. Indeed pigeons will go mad for salt, and can easily overindulge.

In addition to this I always remember my grandmother and mother insisting that the family should have a drink once a week of the water in which any green vegetables had been boiled, claiming that it was one of the finest blood purifiers they knew. I extended this idea to my pigeons, at least once a week introducing a teacupful of this liquid into the 2.8 litre (5pt) water-drinking fountain in the loft. In fact, if it is possible, this should be the first drink given to any birds on their return from a long-distance race, the green water being introduced warm to the fountain so that the water is not ice cold. A little glucose should also be added. The food to accompany this reasonably warm drink, boosted as suggested to replace their energy and clear any impurities they may have picked up, can consist of rice which has been soaked in a little honey dissolved in warm water and allowed to cool. This will swell within the crop and the birds will feel well fed, but their digestion will not be strained and, within an hour or two, even the bird which has faced the toughest of races will be back to its normal self. Many Continental fanciers give a very light diet — called a depurative or cleaning mixture and typically consisting of barley, a little wheat and dari — to pigeons returned from a race. This is gradually replaced, as they build up to the next race, with a mixture rich in carbohydrate from maize, wheat, dari, peas, tares and beans. For young birds a protein-rich mixture is best. Most reputable corn merchants have a range of mixtures for pigeons; indeed some specialise in this trade alone. Their mixtures are very reliable, clean and of good quality grains, and although they cost more than buying individual grains here and there, they are probably worth the extra cost.

Never forget that one reason why the clever fancier controls the quantity of food he supplies, is to make his birds obedient. This does not mean starving them into submission, but rather instilling in them the knowledge that they will get fed if they fly home quickly and trap in unhesitatingly. Once this lesson is learned — and apart from a few idiots pigeons learn quickly — it becomes a conditioned reflex that is always with them. A single whistle, or a rattle on the corn tin, will have the birds tumbling into the loft in a few seconds.

Finally, remember to see that a supply of fresh grit is available to the birds, as they need it to help in the digestion of the corn, and to supply them with calcium to make bone, and eggshell when the hens are laying. Vitamins are present in most good grains, and in green food; no special supply is usually needed. Some fanciers, however, give extra Vitamin B_1 (thiamine), usually in the form of brewer's yeast, because pigeon muscles are very sensitive to the lack of this vitamin — the bird's stock of it can be exhausted in a long hard race, and the bird goes down paralysed.

It is hoped these ideas will illustrate the necessity for studying your birds and their feeding. They echo the words spoken to the author thirty years ago by one of London's most successful fanciers, S.G. Biss, now racing successfully in East Anglia in club, federation, national and international events: 'Master the art of feeding and you are two-thirds of the way to success.'

6
Training

There are so many methods for the training of pigeons that it is almost impossible to lay down set rules on the subject; but this chapter explains, for the newcomer, some of the basic principles involved. It is a subject that causes more heartache to the beginner than any other, for a mistake can so easily cause the loss of several of his best birds.

Training Young Birds

The training of young birds starts almost from birth, certainly from the time they are weaned from their parents. There should be no problem in weaning the young; just place them in their new home, whatever you have selected for them. Some fanciers build a small box or frame of wood within the young-bird section of the loft, whilst others just lean planks or boards against the side of the loft so that the young birds have a corner to run to together and in which to make their home. If it is frosty, put some straw on the floor to keep them warm, for they will not perch at first.

Many prefer a pigeon basket for the purpose of weaning. The young birds can be placed in it through the top flap of the basket, which is well lined with wood chips or coarse sawdust, the main front flap of the basket being left open. After a few minutes the youngsters will be poking their heads through the open front and will soon wander out into the loft and quickly find the water-fountain and food-trough. By nightfall they will all be back in the basket huddled together and sleeping comfortably. The front flap of the basket is then fastened, and when opened again early next morning the youngsters very

A training basket, as recommended for use when weaning young birds (*Rick Osman*)

quickly learn to come out from the basket and seek their food. This can truly be thought of as the beginning of training, because the birds are learning not to have any fear of the basket in later life.

The weaning process is quite short, and within a week to ten days you will find your young birds getting up to the box perches and quickly claiming their own niche within the young-bird loft or section. Spend all the time you can spare with the birds at this period, make them comfortable and happy, play with them, build their confidence in you as their friend.

The basket training can now be carried a stage further for, having had your young birds sleeping in the basket, it is useful to accustom them to feeding and drinking in it as they will have to in case of a delayed liberation in their racing life. With this in mind, after a few nights of sleeping in the basket in the loft, do not open the flap first thing in the morning, but fix a

The ideal: squeakers a week after weaning that are plump, fully feathered, active and bright eyed

water-trough to the outside of the basket and gently pour some water into it from a watering can. Do not fill the trough immediately, but after pouring in a little water stand back and watch. Usually, within a few minutes, one inquisitive bird will poke its head through the aperture and find the water. When this happens, gently drip in more water, and gradually more and more of the birds will begin to drink. After a time you will find that, even when the trough has been removed, some of your youngsters will automatically go towards the opening on the basket where the water-trough should be. This, like everything else connected with pigeon racing, requires patience and should not be regarded as a one-off job; for several weeks, before you actually start on the road, put the water-trough on every time you put your birds in the basket.

The next step is to persuade the youngsters to eat in the basket. To do this, instead of putting the normal feeding-tray in the loft for the evening feed, use a smaller version and put this in the basket. Sprinkle a few grains of corn through the top of the basket on to the tray; when the young birds hear the corn dropping on the tray they will run into the basket. Call or whistle to them every time; for once they have learned there is a connection they will respond to the whistle all their lives. Close the large flap, continue to drop food into the basket among the wood shavings and on to the tray, and you will find the majority of birds will continue to feed. If one or two do not feed on the first occasion, they will come to no harm; next morning they will partake of the light morning feed and that evening, when you repeat the feeding-in-the-basket routine, they will join the others and eat.

At this time you should also encourage your youngsters to move into the external cage or aviary described on p 33. In this way they will obtain a view of the outside of the loft and, if you have your aviary sited correctly, they will have the opportunity to watch your old birds exercising. Then comes the first lesson on trapping into their own section from outside. When the young birds have found their way into the external cage, refix your Anti-bolt wires and quickly call the birds in to feed. They will soon learn to enter the loft from outside.

As soon as possible after this lesson, preferably in the evening on the first few occasions, take away the cage from the let-board and allow the birds to walk around the board or loft top. Have the birds fairly hungry at these times, and they will readily come in when you call them for food. Quite soon the birds will begin to find their wings and take short flaps around the loft, and after about two weeks will begin to fly quite strongly. You should then see the good results of your earlier efforts in calling the birds in from the aviary to food, for when they drop from a fly and are called in immediately to feed they should straight away obey your call. This will save precious moments on many a race day in the future — many prizes are lost because a pigeon comes home in winning time and then dithers on the top of the loft so that it cannot be clocked in.

You must make the birds realise that the end of exercise means food and even possibly a titbit in the form of small seed,

83

one of the best for this purpose being groats. As with children, young birds taught good habits early in life will always follow them. As already mentioned, it is not necessary to starve your birds into obedience — growing young birds must have their proper food — but regular and controlled feeding is essential. It is no good leaving food in the young-bird loft all day, or like children they will be continually nibbling or stuffing and will become over-fat which, in an athlete — and that is what a racing pigeon is — is no use at all.

Our next step with young-bird training is to induce them to realise that, when they leave the basket from outside the loft instead of from inside, their need is to return to the loft and their owner. In this exercise it is useful to have a helper. One evening gently catch each of your birds and place it, using extreme care, into the basket. When they are all inside, carry the basket gently outside the loft and place it on the ground a few feet away. If possible, have a couple of old hen birds, a little on the hungry side, outside the loft on the let-board. With yourself inside the loft, your assistant should gently open the release door of the basket and walk away. Let the young birds walk quietly from the basket just as they have previously done inside the loft. When you see them emerge from the basket, start to call them quietly and drop a few grains of corn on to the feeding-tray. As soon as the birds hear this familiar sound and see the hungry older hens making an effort, they will fly up to the let-board and start to enter the loft, as they have already been taught to do in the cage or aviary stage of training. After repeating this exercise for several days, you can feel reasonably certain that your young birds are comfortably basket-trained and will feel almost as 'at home' in one as they do in the loft.

The first flights of young birds around the loft are full of novelty for them, and anxiety for their owner. They go individually, not in a tight flock, avoiding collisions by hair-breadths. They are easily picked up by passing flocks of race birds, so avoid weekends for their first outings if at all possible. Once the young birds have taken off from the loft and begin to batch together, flying for a period of about half an hour, it is time to think about their road-training tosses. For the first session, put them in the basket just as before, remembering to handle them carefully and talking to each one individually as you place it in. Your helper should then take the birds about 1 mile away and very quietly release them after a pause of 12–20 minutes. You will probably find that the birds will go for their normal fly of about half an hour, but as they will have been circling round the loft, you will see them within that time. Do not call them immediately you see them, but as soon as they show signs of dropping into the loft be there to call them in gently to food. Remember with young birds the maxim for good training is 'out of the basket, home to food and their friend, their owner'.

Repeat this one-mile exercise about three times, then step up the distance to 10 miles (16km) and repeat this three or four times. On each occasion the birds should, depending on the weather conditions, improve on the previous time by which they appeared over the loft, but, because they are still young birds and keen to fly, will continue flying around home for their normal time. After three tosses at 10 miles (16km)

A training toss — six pigeons released from a basket to fly home

increase the distance to 20 miles (32km) and have two or three tosses from this point. Then, after two or three from 30 miles (48km) your young birds should be ready to compete in their first race.

It is important to carry out these training tosses in reasonable weather conditions, so consult the weather forecasts. Avoid cold easterly winds or dense cloud cover, and if there is a possibility of fog, heavy rain or thunder your birds are better off in the loft at home.

The objects of training are two-fold: firstly, to train the muscles and organs of the pigeon's body for the tasks we expect it to undertake; secondly, to accustom the bird to the countryside over which you expect it to fly. This is why, on the earlier shorter tosses, you will find the birds take as long to home as they do when the distances become longer — in the earlier spins they have been searching and growing used to the terrain over which they travel, and developing their sense of orientation.

Do not cram all your training tosses into too short a period. By all means train on consecutive days if the weather and your time permit; but try to give the birds the odd day at home between tosses, otherwise they may become tired of the basket or begin to think that it, more than the loft, is their home. Remember our motto: 'We must create in our birds a love of their own home.'

It is worth stressing that you should do your very best to select fair flying days. The birds will run into bad weather conditions during their racing careers, but there is no reason to face these conditions unnecessarily. Remember young birds are still growing and are still quite immature; their self-confidence is easily shaken. The successful fancier is the one who is considerate to his birds, particularly in conserving their energy at all times, and who has their health and welfare always uppermost in his mind. The good fancier will always give the bird the benefit of the doubt if there is the slightest question in his mind about its fitness to accomplish a certain task he may be asking of it.

Training Old Birds

So far we have discussed youngsters, but what of the old birds? The task here is not quite so difficult because older birds will have been racing during the previous season or seasons, so training them over the ground is not as important since they will already have covered the area a number of times. If your old birds have been flying reasonably well at home during February and March, they will have begun to exercise their muscles and body organs, so what they really need is mental exercise. This is because they have been largely resting during the winter months and, even if they have been able to venture out for exercise on fine days, their flights have become somewhat routine to them. The object of short training tosses for old birds prior to the first race of the season in late April is therefore to make them use their brains again, to remind them that their objective is to leave the basket or crate in which they are sent to the training point and to return home, back to the comfort of their loft and the company of their owner.

About 15 miles (24km) for the first training toss is about right; after they have been to that point a couple of times, the old birds can be lifted to a 20 mile (32km) stage. But make sure you pick the right days for training. The object is mental stimulus, but it will be a fruitless exercise if you send the birds away on dirty or sticky days and make them start to worry about the elements.

When should one start training old birds? This must depend on your race programme, but if the weather is favourable it is useful to arrange the first couple of shorter spins whilst the birds are sitting on the first clutch of eggs. I have never liked training birds whilst they are rearing their first young birds of the season. That time of year is one of the most enjoyable of all — seeing your old birds happy and contented and raising their young seems to bring you closer than ever to your birds.

Yearlings can be very tricky to train, especially the cocks.

Full of the energy of youth, they can go crazy when sent off to the first training toss, and may fly right past their loft and on for 200 miles (322km) or so before checking. It is probably safer to send yearlings when sitting, and never when the cock is driving his hen to lay.

One final point on the subject of training, don't forget that notebook. Do not rely on your memory, but make a note of how the birds come in from training spins, whether one or two were outstanding and, if so, what was their condition. Were they sitting eggs, feeding young birds or, in the case of cocks, calling the hen to nest again? What was it that made them that much better than the remainder of the team on that particular day? This is all part of our own training as fanciers. We cannot store knowledge about our birds purely in our minds — human memory is too fickle.

7

Selection for Racing and the Natural System

Let us now turn our attention to racing our pigeons. You will by now, almost certainly, have joined your local club or society, have attended club meetings and race markings (see pp108–9), and have been generally learning all you can about the sport. One point must be emphasised from the start — you should give the same attention to the later arrivals from races as you do to the first because, if you have done your part before sending the birds to the race, they will give of their best for you and your last bird one week could easily be the first the next.

Old-bird racing includes all birds carrying a ring issued by a recognised union or association in the years prior to that particular season. Young-bird racing includes only birds bred and ringed with official rings issued in the current year. In most British organisations the rings are not issued until about 10 January to make sure, it is claimed, that birds with rings of that year must have been bred in that year. I have also heard it is said that this date originated about 1910 with the first registration rings in this country, which were sold by the weekly newspaper *The Racing Pigeon*. Its then editor, Lt Col A.H. Osman, who was in charge of the Army Pigeon services during World War I, decided that the ring was the pigeon's birth certificate and would be issued on his son's birthday. (Incidentally, this son, Major W.H. Osman, succeeded his father as editor of the paper which is still being published today — its eighty-sixth year — and is still edited by a member of the Osman family, the major's son, Colin.)

Physical Fitness

Younger enthusiasts or newcomers to the sport inevitably ask how can they tell when a pigeon is fit or in condition. The only answer is that a fancier must keep his eyes and ears open for 365 days a year. A bird which is off colour or below par will, like a human being, in nine cases out of ten show it in the eye. If a bird is fit, the eye should be sparkling and throw a gleam; but if a bird's eye looks dull and lack-lustre it is not in the best condition and something is wrong, probably internally. Feathering is another clearly visible sign. If a bird is in condition, the feathering will be beautifully smooth and silky, and the neck feathers with their extraordinarily beautiful colours will glow and radiate brightness. In a bird not quite up to standard this glow of fitness will disappear and the neck feathers will become loose; in fact the whole feathering will seem lack-lustre.

Another important visual sign is the bird's wattle — the spongy or honeycomb-like material above the bird's beak. If a bird is in good health this should be white in colour; if it appears dull-grey or greasy, this is a dangerous sign and every care should be taken to see that this bird is not sent to a race or subjected to any physical strain.

So far, we have been talking about general physical fitness; it is essential also to take into account any special factor regarding a particular bird. For instance, in the case of a hen bird, even if she appears perfectly fit and healthy it would be wrong to send her to a race and subject her to undue physical strain either immediately before or immediately after laying.

Old Birds and the Natural System

The selection of birds for entry in the various races is the first problem. Pigeons are indeed athletes, and there are successful strains or families for racing short or longer distances; nowadays birds are advertised as being sprint, middle or long distance. It is important for the novice or newcomer to the sport to realise that winners of races from 500 miles (805km) will seldom, if ever, have descended from a family of birds which has only been successful up to say, 250 miles (400km). With this in mind, a successful pigeon fancier will plan his season, and the birds he intends to send on longer races will be earmarked early, say mid-March to mid-April, and mated accordingly. This will give time for the moult to progress far enough for the birds to have as near as possible a full wing when the longer races arrive. For a bird destined for a 800 mile (1,287km) event — and probably it will be a third-season bird or older — mating should take place about the second week in March.

Old birds are in this country generally raced on what is known as the Natural System, that is when the birds are mated, reared and bred as naturally as possible, and both cocks and hens raced. Under this system it is noticeable that few, if any, birds begin to show signs of fitness until after casting the first primary flight feathers. This is usually after the rearing of the first clutch of young birds, and when the parent birds have been comfortably sitting for eight to ten days on their second round of eggs. There is a slight variation between the various strains, but it can be assumed as a firm guideline that most pigeons will not show real attributes for racing until after the first primaries have been cast.

The main object for most fanciers is success in the longer races, and although winning shorter events is gratifying, they are, providing their birds are racing consistently well in the shorter races, generally quite happy to treat these as training spins, helping to develop the birds physically and mentally for the longer events. Just as a marathon runner will not go out and run the punishing 26 miles (42km) straight off but will have several shorter runs, gradually increasing the distance and building up his muscles and stamina, so it should be with our long-distance birds. Therefore the pigeons that are intended to do long journeys should have a programme mapped out for them which will steadily but surely build them up mentally and physically for maximum performance.

Racing of old birds under the Natural System means that you must be observant in your loft and note down the particular characteristics of individual pigeons with regard to readiness for racing. Some birds will race well after sitting on eggs for a week, others on eggs that are just chipping, some when they are feeding young birds about a week old and yet others when they have a single big youngster to feed. However, as a generalisation, there should be few problems if you plan to race them when they have been sitting for four to fourteen days, for they will have recovered from laying but will not have reached the time of formation of soft food in the crop.

Few, if any, fanciers race absolutely natural because, as previously explained, the rearing of young birds is a strain on the parents. So many fanciers deviate slightly and allow their birds to rear only a single young bird in the second nest, and from the third nest onwards race the birds dry; in other words the real eggs are replaced with imitation or 'pot' eggs which, as already mentioned, are obtainable in chalk, china and even plastic. Again it is important to keep your notebook to hand, making records of when the hen lays and you replace the eggs. Such notes will enable you to compare the condition of fitness of your individual pigeons at any one time.

Many fanciers also say, and in most cases I agree, that it is wrong to send either a cock or a hen racing during the first three or four days after their youngsters have hatched. However, I had one hen bird which raced most successfully and won all her positions when put in the racing basket the day her youngsters hatched, though this was accidental. It happened because, working late one evening, I asked my son to put two particular birds in the basket ready for me to send to a race from the 300 mile (483km) stage. By the time I arrived home, the birds had been taken to the marking station and they had been race marked. Then, visiting the loft later in the evening as usual, I discovered the cock mated to this particular hen feeding two youngsters. I had failed in my notes and slipped up in my calculations so that, instead of sending the hen, as I thought, to race home on the day her young birds were due to hatch, they had hatched the day she went away. I was most surprised when, the birds having been released on the Sunday following a day's holdover due to bad weather, this bird homed in time to win the race. Unfortunately, however, there was one of those mishaps which can occur to pigeon fanciers — for the first time in my life the clock stopped, the bird was penalised and did not take the position. However, this particular hen went on later to win several more prizes and on those occasions her condition was always the same in that her eggs hatched just prior to basketing for the race.

Probably the best pigeon I ever owned was a Blue Chequer pied cock, which won seventeen positions in spite of the fact that in every case the race was just at the time when he was looking to or calling his hen to nest. And these are just two examples of the necessity for observation and the fact that the successful fancier is the one who spots details, notes them and is prepared to act upon them.

'Horses for courses' is another of my pet theories, and if I owned a pigeon that won from certain race points I would plan to keep that particular bird for those particular races. For example, the Blue Chequer pied cock mentioned won ten of his prizes from 100 miles (161km) and 300 miles (483km). One very successful fancier told me I would never win with him from 500 miles (805km) and my reply was, 'Why bother to try when he is continually scoring from 100 to 300 miles?'

Yearlings
Still under the heading of old birds, you should take care and use discretion on racing yearlings. Do not send them every week to the bitter end. Many owners of pigeons will disagree with me on this, but yearlings are still developing and one would not ask a schoolboy to undertake a man's job. I know one successful fancier who has never raced yearling hens because, when such birds were rearing their first-season youngsters, they were undergoing internal changes and development of their organs, and would be all the better for a

restful season with just a few short training spins. That doyen of pigeon fanciers and writers, F.W.S. Hall of Enfield, has said on several occasions that if at the end of your first season of old-bird racing you have a team of yearlings which, under your control, have obtained experience related to their physical abilities, the outlook for you in the sport is rosy.

Racing of Young Birds

The racing of young birds (birds hatched in the same year), is easy compared with the problems and anxieties which can arise with older birds. Once you have trained them, they are generally raced unpaired and so the worries of egg laying, hatching, etc, do not occur. There are fanciers who believe it pays to race young birds paired, but I do not think this is generally of benefit to the birds, for young birds raced mated do not develop well later.

However, having said that, you may have a particularly precocious young cock bird and find that the best way to quieten him down is to find him an old hen who will encourage him and keep him quiet. But at all costs do not allow young hens to lay. Some fanciers will disagree and tell you they have won races with young hens which have laid and raced to their eggs; but they never tell you of any success with these birds later in life and it must be remembered that it is this year's young birds which provide the champions of the future.

In connection with racing young birds, it is wise to stop one or two of those which have raced well up to, say 100–120 miles (160–193km), to save them for next year whilst the others can go to the end of the programme, the longest young bird races in most organisations in Britain being around 200 miles (322km).

To sum up, in selecting birds for any race the important thing is physical fitness and, next to that, the stage the bird is at in its life-cycle. To achieve success in racing you need a great deal of patience to learn the individual traits and preferences of each one of your birds, and it is worth stressing again that by keeping your numbers within reasonable limits you will be far more likely to attain your objective. Quality not quantity is important; after all it only takes one pigeon to win a race.

8
Other
Successful Racing Systems

It was said, in the last chapter, that the Natural System of racing is the one most generally used in this country. Other fanciers, however, follow special systems which they believe lead to success, although one wonders if it really is the system or the person behind it.

The Widowhood System

On the Continent most fanciers adopt the Widowhood System of racing which means, in essence, that they only race cocks. In recent years this system has found an increasing number of followers in this country, but it is still noticeable that the leading birds from longer-distance races in Great Britain include a large number of hens. Basically, in this system, after pairing and the rearing of the first nest of youngsters, the cocks only see their mates just prior to or just after returning from a training spin or race — hence the name 'widowhood'. The fanciers who practise this system say the work involved in bringing pigeons to, or keeping them in, a fit condition for racing, is far less worrying than under the Natural System. Nevertheless, practically the same amount of time must be spent with the birds because, whatever system one adopts, exercise, attention to cleanliness, regular feeding and supplying of fresh water are absolute essentials.

The complete system is as follows. The birds are mated in mid- or late-December and, after they have reared the first nest of youngsters and have settled down on their second clutch of eggs, the hens are taken away from the loft, the young birds weaned and the cocks left sitting on the eggs which they will neglect after about two days. From this stage onwards the cock is alone and comfortable in his own nest-box which is also his perch, there being no other in the loft. The cocks are exercised regularly for at least an hour each day, after which they return to the loft and are fed and watered, each in his own nest-box. Often darkness is achieved by louvre blinds lowered in front of the loft so that the cock birds will be completely at rest; there will be no flying and no fighting.

When training begins the hen is introduced into the nest-box but on the other side of a dividing partition, so that the cock can see the hen but cannot have contact with her. On return from a training toss the cock is allowed in the box with the hen for a very short time, but as soon as he begins to nuzzle her or gently coo or call to her, the hen is removed until the next time the cock is basketed either for training or racing. Some fanciers, after the first nest of young birds have been

Widowhood cocks enjoy their daily feed in a spotlessly clean compartment

After feeding, each cock goes back to his own box

weaned and the hens removed, leave the nest-bowl in the box but turned upside down. Then, when the cocks are out exercising or on a training spin, they turn the bowls up the correct way and introduce the hen, so that when the cock returns the hen is standing in the nest-bowl. After a period of this sort of encouragement, it has been known for fanciers to race a team of cocks very successfully without introducing the hens before the cocks go away; the mere turning of the nest-bowl will give the cocks the urge to return because they know that the hens will be in the boxes in the bowls awaiting them.

What does seem strange about the system is that, if followed rigidly, only cocks are raced. For the strength of the strain of birds in a loft lies with the hens, and one cannot possibly judge their quality unless they are subjected to some racing. It is no good breeding pigeons for racing from unknown performers; one must at least use pigeons of known performances within a generation or so. I was therefore very interested when the late Maurice Henrotin, a former Secretary of the Fédération Colombophile Internationale (see Chapter 13), mentioned in conversation once a system of widowhood racing for hens. Maurice wrote an article on Belgian racing every year for some thirty years in *Squill's Year Book*, an annual published by *The Racing Pigeon*, which includes articles by leading fanciers of the year. In 'Widowhood Method for Hens', the last of his articles written just before he died, he outlined this system; because it is a method which a fancier with quite a small loft could adopt, it is summarised as follows.

The method has produced outstanding results but has to be followed very strictly. The loft is divided into two sections (loft No 1 and loft No 2) which must be absolutely identical — same dimensions, same type of nest-boxes in identical positions, same colouring on the walls and the same feeding and watering arrangements in identical places; the idea being that whichever loft a bird is in, it will recognise the loft and its own nest-box.

In February the pigeons are paired in No 1 loft and rear one round of youngsters. After the laying of the second clutch of eggs the hens are trained over short distances. After ten days the hens only are transferred to No 2 loft, where they will immediately take to nest-boxes as in No 1 loft. The real training begins a few days after this separation, the cocks being exercised for an hour in the morning and in the evening. When the cocks return from the evening fly to loft No 1, the hens are released for exercise for one hour; at the same time the cocks are moved to loft No 2 where they will be fed, watered and spend the night in the box to which they will immediately take as identical to their box in loft No 1. The hens meanwhile have returned to loft No 1 and are fed and watered and spend the night there in the identical nest-box to that in loft No 2. Next morning the cocks are released for exercise and, whilst they are away, the hens are moved into No 2 loft to the same boxes as in loft No 1 and so on. By using this method the cocks exercise two hours a day and the hens one hour, but after exercise or training the birds always return to

No 1 loft. Cocks and hens can be raced each weekend in short- or middle-distance races, but not in the same race.

Although this method gives really outstanding results, it demands a great deal of attention from the fancier, because if a bird should discover the transfer from loft No 1 to loft No 2 the results would be nil. Besides this, the fancier has to take the birds individually and slowly to the same nest-box in loft No 2 where they are always fed.

The Celibacy System

Many years ago that great fancier, Dr M.E. Tresidder, wrote an article entitled 'The Celibacy System'. This, he pointed out, did not involve any sensual or sexual urge and was very simple to operate. Basically it entails the complete parting of the cocks and hens after the rearing of the first round of young birds, and in keeping them apart for the rest of the racing season. This system can be worked in a normal loft with two or more compartments, the important difference being that the partitions are solid and opaque so that the birds cannot kiss or beak or see each other through them. Those who practise this system say that both sexes exercise and fly well. It does not occupy as much time as the Natural System (see Chapter 7), but a drawback seems to be that all the birds are treated as a team; it does not allow for the individuality of the pigeons.

The Jealousy System

Another system which some fanciers have success with is based on jealousy. It is also time-consuming, the basis being to provide two mates for a cock or a hen. Supposing you wish to prepare two cocks for racing under this system; you need to choose a particularly amorous hen and for the first couple of days allow her in the nest-box with cock No 1. Then you have to remove this cock from the loft and, after a few hours, introduce cock No 2. On the day of despatch to a race, close the nest-box with cock No 2 in the box with the hen, and let cock No 1 back into the loft where he will fly straight to the front of the box, see the apparent interloper and be anxious to oust him. At the same time cock No 2 will regard No 1 as the interloper and be just as keen to oust him. Do not let them fight but remove them one at a time to the basket for sending to the race. The basket will have to be of show type where the birds are completely separated. The cocks race home faster, because each believes the other is still with the mate he desires. The procedure is, of course, reversed in the case of two hens and one cock.

There is one danger in this method as a very old friend of mine found out. He had prepared two cocks in this manner, and on the race day they arrived home together in time to win; but they decided to settle their differences on the top of the loft and so lost the race. Also, in the scrap both cocks damaged their flights, and he was unable to race either any more that season.

The results of fighting: three primaries are so damaged that this bird will not race this season

An extension of this system was practised by the late Joe Morrison — a very successful fancier in north London in the 1940s and 1950s. Joe had some extra large nest-boxes in which he had as many as four hens paired naturally to one cock. Each hen had her own nest-bowl in a corner of the box and sat naturally, the cock taking his turn sitting with any of the four hens. During the week prior to the race Joe would gradually move the nest-bowls nearer to each other until, on the day of basketing for the race, the bowls were almost touching. During this time the hens were beginning to take notice of each other and there might be an occasional flap of the wing one against the other. When all four hens were put in the basket for race marking, the thought of the other hens aroused their maternal instincts and they raced home very successfully the next day.

Systems for Young Birds

All the ideas mentioned so far refer to racing old birds. Regarding young birds, as was stated earlier, I prefer to see them racing naturally to their own perches. But in Belgium and other Continental countries, fanciers usually breed young birds in December, ring them very early in January and pair them before racing them. This is claimed to bring racing success; but nevertheless, unmated later-bred young birds win the longer National Young Birds events in Belgium.

One system for young-bird racing which can prove very successful is to keep the sexes in separate compartments of the loft all week between races, and then let them run together just before basketing for the race. There may be the odd young bird whose sex is difficult to determine, but generally if a young cock bird is among the group of hens he will begin to show himself a little quicker.

All this talk of various systems should not divert you from the fact that no system will make a bad pigeon into a good one, but it might make a good pigeon better. The skill of the fancier in imparting to the pigeon the extra will and energy to fly home quickly is what wins races, especially at short and medium distances. In long races of over 500 miles (805km) or more, the quality of the bird is more important than the art of the owner or the system that he follows.

9
Organisation of Pigeon Races

In addition to the many mature adults, both men and women, who are starting to keep pigeons these days, it is pleasing to note that there are many younger people coming into the sport and even schools are starting lofts to help interested youngsters. But the question which seems to puzzle all such newcomers is how the results in a pigeon race can be decided. On television they can see how easy it is, for instance, in a horse race, where the horses start together and all finish at the same place. It is the same in most other race events; but in pigeon racing, although they all start from the same place, each bird is homing to its own loft. How, therefore, can it be decided which bird is the winner?

Briefly, the winner is the bird which covers the journey from the liberation point to its home loft at the highest average speed, the distance being calculated on what is known as the Great Circle System — an extremely complicated formula which allows for the curvature of the surface of the earth. The time at which the birds are released from the race point is known; they then race home where each one is timed by means of a special clock at its own loft, and the average speed is calculated in yards per minute.

But the question still remains: 'How do you know which bird has arrived home first?' The answer is that, prior to the bird being despatched to the point of liberation, it has a rubber ring attached to its leg by means of a special ringing machine which cannot harm its foot. This rubber ring carries code numbers, one on the outside of the ring and one on the inside. The outside number is noted by the club committee and recorded on the competitor's entry form against the

A Benzing clock showing the time record tape being removed (*Rick Osman*)

number of the metal identity-ring which was placed on the
bird's leg soon after hatching (see pp 56–7). The entry form is
retained by the club. Each of these rubber rings has a paper
duplicate which contains the same numbers; and both rubber
ring and paper duplicate remain secret until after the bird has
been clocked in by its owner from the race. These numbers are
then compared by officials and must agree; if they do not, the
pigeon will not be allowed to take its position in the event.

But even with these precautions, an obvious source of
unfairness arises if one fancier's clock should be slow,
another's fast and yet another's correct by the time the race is
finished. The pigeon of the man with the slow clock would
appear to have flown the journey quicker, whilst that of the
man with the fast clock would appear to have taken longer for
the journey. The problem is overcome by a system of compen-
sating for such errors, the starting point of which is that every

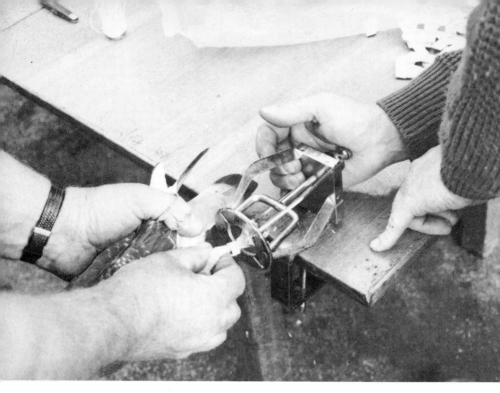

Basketing night: the coded rubber ring goes on to the pigeon's leg

Into the pannier, and the pointer moves up one place

The basket is sealed with a numbered metal disc and string

The numbers of the seals are recorded

competitor must possess his own clock of a special type approved by the organisation which is running the sport in his area. The design of these clocks is such that they can only be opened by authorised members of the clock committee, or by the clock setter as the man in charge is known. He is in possession of the master clock which is synchronised with Greenwich Mean Time (GMT) — or, rather, since most racing takes place during the summer, British Summer Time (BST) — and any variation of this master clock is taken into consideration and calculated accurately. Every competitor's clock is controlled through the master clock and any variation by the competitor's clock is also calculated accurately.

Over the years there has been a great improvement in the quality of these clocks and now, in the micro-chip age, there are many on the market where any variation that occurs during the time the clock is normally used by a pigeon racer is so small as to be of no account. Many modern quartz models will run for a long period without variation

After the bird's arrival time has been noted and its code numbers scrutinised by the clock setter or clock committee, variations are calculated for each clock where necessary so that the exact corrected time of every bird's arrival is known. The committee, generally led by the club secretary, then proceed with the calculation of the average speed — colloquially known as the bird's 'velocity' — of each bird over the journey. The velocities are then arranged in order and the bird recording the highest velocity is declared the winner, the next highest declared second, and so on down the list. The arrival of the micro-chip pocket calculator has considerably eased the work of club secretaries and clock setters, and some of the larger organisations now own computers which present the result from the information obtained. However, consideration of the calculations as they were done before the advent of calculators, will explain how the system works.

Adjustments to the Clocks

The first step, as already explained, is synchronisation of the clocks. In order that the clock setter or clock committee can adjust every competitor's clock to the master clock, all clocks are submitted to these officials at the beginning of the season and undergo running tests. They then remain in the possession of the club throughout the racing season, except when a race is on, although a member may transfer his clock under official seal from one club to another.

Each week during the racing season, on the day the birds are despatched, the master clock is set correct against a time signal from BBC radio or GPO Speaking Clock. From this master clock all competitors' clocks are set and then, at a given time, are operated, or 'struck', with each competitor striking another member's clock, and the clock setter operating the master clock to record the time. This bulk striking of clocks is known as the 'setting time'. The clocks are now ready for use by the competitors, and each will then take his own home to await the arrival of his birds from the race. He will then clock them in as they arrive by taking the rubber ring from each pigeon and putting it into the clock. He then takes his clock to the club headquarters. The master clock is again checked with BBC or GPO, and any variation noted. Each competitor's clock is then struck again with the master clock — the 'checking time' — and any variation between the two clocks recorded.

It is now possible, by removing the dials or printed rolls, to know the time at which the competitor's clock was originally set, and checking with the master clock will have shown whether the former has run either fast or slow. This total gain or loss is noted and then the proportionate gain or loss up to the time that the bird was clocked in is calculated and an adjustment made. In this calculation the interval from setting time to checking time is known as the 'long run', and the time from setting to the clocking in of the bird is the 'short run'. The formula for adjustment is a simple proportion:

$$\frac{\text{Short run in seconds}}{\text{Long run in seconds}} \times \text{gain or loss in seconds}$$

This variation must be calculated for the master clock first to ascertain the correct setting time (the time at which the competitors' clocks were synchronised with the master clock), then a similar calculation has to be made for each competitor's clock. In some of the longer or harder races where the birds may be clocked as much as an hour or more apart, a calculation may be necessary for each bird clocked. Allowance for any error in the setting is then adjusted to bring the time in line with the master clock.

The following are a few examples of actual calculations. We will assume that the birds were race-marked on a Friday and the race flown the next day:

1   Master Clock

		Time on Clock	*Radio Time*	*Corrected Time*
Friday	Radio set	6.00pm	6.00pm	
	Members' set	8.00pm		8.03pm
Saturday	Radio check	5.59.24pm	6.00pm	
	Members' check	7.59.24pm		8.03pm

It will be seen that the master clock has lost 36sec in 24hr. To adjust the time of setting members' clocks on Friday we must make this calculation:

6.00pm – 8.00pm = 2hr (short run)
6.00pm – 6.00pm = 24hr (long run)
Total loss = 36sec

$$\frac{2 \times 36}{24} = 3 \text{ sec}$$

Thus by 8pm on Friday the master clock had lost 3sec and the corrected time of setting competitors' clocks is 8.03pm.

On Saturday two hours elapsed after checking the master clock against radio time and so we have another calculation to make. We know the clock lost 36sec in 24hr; now we have to fix the loss in 26hr:

110

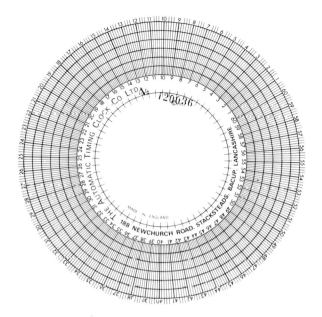

Fig 9　The minute dial as used on the Toulet puncturing-type clock

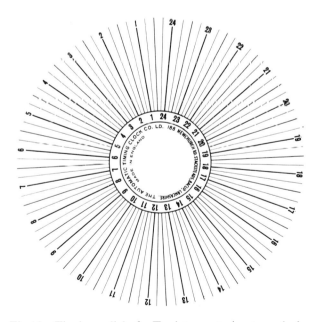

Fig 10　The hour dial of a Toulet puncturing-type clock

111

$$\frac{26 \times 36}{24} = 39sec$$

Thus the corrected time for checking competitors' clocks was 7.59.24 + 39sec which brings it to 8.03pm.

2 Competitor No 1 (clock running slow when set correct)

	Time on Clock	Correct Time	Corrected Time
Friday set	8.03pm	8.03pm	
Saturday: bird clocked	2.14.27pm		2.15.58pm
Saturday check	7.58.3pm	8.03pm	

Long run = 23hr 58min
Short run = 18hr 14min 24sec
Total loss = 120sec

Applying the formula of p110 and working in seconds we have:

$$\text{Variation } \frac{65664 \times 120}{86280} = \frac{787968}{8628} = 91.3sec$$

So that 91sec have to be added to the time on the clock making 2.15.58pm.

To make the figures quite clear, the clock was struck against the master clock at setting at 8.03pm and the clock was reading 8.03pm. When synchronised with the master clock on Saturday at 8.03pm the clock in fact showed 7.58.3 (two minutes slow), and so the clock has lost 120sec in 24hr.

3 Competitor No 2 (clock running fast when set correct)

	Time on Clock	Correct Time	Corrected Time
Friday set	8.03pm	8.03pm	
Saturday: bird clocked	2.17.29pm		2.15.58pm
Saturday check	8.2.3pm	8.03pm	

Long run = 24hr 2min
Short run = 18hr 17min 26sec
Total gain = 120 sec

$$\text{Variation } \frac{65846 \times 120}{86520} = \frac{790152}{8652} = 91.3\text{sec}$$

Thus 91sec must be taken from clock time. This clock has gained 120sec; when checked against the master clock it was 2 min 120sec fast.

4 Competitor No 3 (clock set fast, then running slow)

	Time on Clock	Correct Time	Corrected Time
Friday set	8.0.13pm	8.03pm	
Saturday: bird			
clocked	2.14.27pm		2.15.56.pm
Saturday check	7.58.3pm	8.0.3pm	

Long run = 23hr 57min 50sec
Short run = 18hr 14min 14sec
Total loss = 130sec

$$\text{Variation } \frac{65654 \times 130}{86270} = 98.9$$

To the nearest second this means 99sec to be added to clock time, but 10sec (the amount the clock was set fast) has to be deducted giving a net 89sec to be added. Corrected time is therefore 2.15.56pm.

To again clarify the position: this clock was 10sec fast when synchronised with the master clock at setting, and when synchronised after the race was 120sec slow, so that the total loss during the long run was 130sec, but an allowance must then be made for the 10sec it was set fast, after calculating the loss variation.

5 Competitor No 4 (clock set slow, then running fast)

	Time on Clock	Correct Time	Corrected Time
Friday set	7.59.53pm	8.03pm	
Saturday: bird			
clocked	2.17.29pm		2.16.0pm
Saturday check	8.2.3pm	8.03pm	

Long run = 24hr 2min 10sec
Short run = 18hr 17min 36sec
Total gain = 130sec

$$\text{Variation } \frac{65856 \times 130}{86530} = 98.9\text{sec}$$

To the nearest second this means 99sec to be taken off the time, but adjustment must be made for the time set slow (10sec); therefore the amount to be deducted is 89sec. This clock has gained; it was 10sec slow at setting; 120 sec fast at checking.

Calculation of Average Speed (Velocity)

Now to ascertain speed. Every competitor will have had the exact location of his loft marked with a small pin-prick by club officials on the most up-to-date Ordnance Survey map of the area. This map is then sent to an official calculator who, using an officially approved formula, calculates the distance from each officially located liberation point to the loft. This distance is given in miles and yards, then reduced to sixtieths of a yard, and the flying time is reduced to seconds; thus, by dividing the time taken into the distance flown, the speed is calculated in yards per minute. 'Flying time' means the time from the moment of the liberation to the time that the bird is clocked in (the corrected times as previously calculated after correcting for clock variation). The time at which the bird was liberated from the race point is given by the convoyer (see Chapter 11).

Let us, as an example, look at the previously quoted competitor No 2. The corrected time of arrival was 2.15.58pm, and we will assume that the liberation time was given by the convoyer as 8.00am and that the distance was 198 miles 282yd. Flying time is therefore 6hr 15min 58sec.

It can easily be calculated that the average speed is about 31½mph, but this is not accurate enough and so we work it out as already mentioned:

Distance
198 miles reduced to 60ths of a yard = 20908800
282yd reduced to 60ths of a yard   =   16920

                                     _____
                                        20925720
                                     _____

114

Flying Time
6hr 15min 58sec = 22558sec

Thus to find the bird's velocity we have to divide 20925720 by 22558, which makes the bird's speed 927.64yd per minute.

Most clubs do not go to more than two places of decimals, for it is officially recognised that the formula used for calculating measurements of distance, although the best to date, is not totally accurate. In fact it is only guaranteed to give accuracy to within 100ft. In addition there is the possibility of some small error in the location of the loft, particularly if clubs still use the old 6in OS maps and not the latest 50in plans now available. Personally I have always believed that, under the present accuracy of calculation, birds recording the same speed to one place of decimals should be regarded as a dead-heat.

IO

Shows and Exhibitions

Preparing the Birds

One aspect of our racing-pigeon sport which has grown over recent years is the show or exhibition. Years ago this was regarded rather as a sideline and only a couple of major shows were held during the winter months, with local clubs organising smaller shows among their members to provide social get-togethers during the non-racing season. Today the interest in Show Racer breeding and showing has increased to such an extent that there are organisations which specialise in just that, under the title of Show Racer societies. I have a great respect for those who enjoy this side of the sport, for their dedication in preparing birds for the classic show season is no less than that of the racing fancier who plans and works so hard to prepare a bird for a 5–600 mile (804–966km) race.

There used to be a great difference between the pigeons produced by show specialists and the racing pigeon; the show specimens of those days being often described as Show Homers. But today the Show Racer, through the concentrated efforts and devotion of enthusiasts in the matter of careful breeding and selection, has become a sleeker-bodied pigeon with a body shape, head, balance and quality of feather that is outstanding. There are certain racing-pigeon men who, when they act as judges at shows, immediately condemn a bird they think is a Show Racer. This is totally wrong. In my opinion all pigeons in a show must be judged on merit in accordance with a particular class. For example, if the class is for birds which have flown say 400 miles (644km), it is up to the show organisers to satisfy themselves that the bird has flown the required distance and for the judge to give his decision on that

116

basis, not to walk past saying such things as, 'That's a show bird, it would never fly so far'.

Many show birds can fly the necessary distance, if they are given the chance, and this has been proved over the years. Probably one of the most successful racing strains used in the development of the Show Racer was the Gurnay — the successful racing strain of Renier Gurnay of Belgium — which was particularly good looking and which raced extremely well for fanciers in Great Britain and on the Continent, particularly between the two world wars. The other great strain was the Dordin, developed by that doyen of racing in France, the late Pierre Dordin, on whose birds the original International Standard was established after World War II (see Chapter 13).

There is no recognised official standard for judging Show Racers, but in most judges' opinion, the bird should not have too big a body. The keel should not be too deep or too long and should curve upwards slightly towards the vent; it should also be quite smooth and straight with no dents or bumps. The bird should have a reasonable amount of flesh and muscles — flesh, not fat. A bird which is fat and flabby will be immediately discounted. To use a common term among pigeon fanciers, the pigeon should be 'apple-bodied'. The back is also of great importance; it should be firm and straight and flat through to the seat of the tail, with no sign of a dip down. The tail should not go up when the bird is being handled and, as with the ordinary racing pigeon, the bird should be well-balanced in the hand.

The wing, when opened or fanned, is a point of difference between the show and the racing pigeon. Many fanciers believe that, for successful racing, pigeons should have a distinct step between the secondaries and the first primaries. But it is accepted that in the Show Racer the wing should be even, showing only a gentle curve from the body to the tip of the last primary flight. The web of the primary flight should be wide and the quills strong; the secondaries and small coverts should cover the back well, not leaving a wide gap towards the tail. As for lengths of flights, the primaries should

117

How to hold a pigeon and inspect its wing

finish about ¾in (20mm) from the end of the tail feathers, which should be strong and clean, any signs of soiling in the loft having been carefully washed away before the bird is exhibited.

The flights and tail feathers should be free from fretmarks and small pin-holes, a fretmark being a light-coloured line or wave across the flight indicating deficiency in the basic colour of the feathering. It is usually caused by some strain or stress, and means that the feathers have been deprived of nourishment during their growing period. For instance, a bird which has had an extremely hard fly over a long distance, or missed its journey home and spent a night or so away from its loft without food, will have used all its resources in its flying and the growing feather will have been starved. Young birds may show fretmarks from the nest stage if they have not been properly fed by the adult birds. However, provided all else is physically right, these fretmarks will disappear if the bird goes correctly through its first moult.

The classic show season usually runs from late October through to about mid-January, and with more and more shows being organised there is sometimes an unfortunate clash of dates. Top show enthusiasts then face the dilemma of whether to split their team between two events or to exhibit at the show at which they feel their team has the best chance of winning. The decision involves consideration of the birds' records; therefore it is as vital for the show fancier to be observant and note all details about his loft as it is for the racing pigeon fancier. With no set standard for the Show Racer, there are various likes and dislikes among judges. The clever show man will therefore note the particular colour or type of bird which a judge has shown leanings towards in the past, and will use this in deciding where and when to show his birds.

As with a racing loft, the show man must be with his pigeons for some time every day of the year and if this is not possible he must have someone else to help. Only constant attention to the birds all the year round will build a team and raise the birds to peak condition at the date of a particular show. As with racers, it is important to be as regular as possible in all activities in the loft. Cleanliness is even more important than for the racing-pigeon man in that the perches must be set in such a way that droppings from one bird soiling the feathering of the bird below is kept to a minimum. Alternatively, special perches can be used (see p 33).

As with a team of pigeons for racing, so with a team of show birds, one of the greatest dangers is overcrowding of the loft. Never keep more birds for exhibition than you can house properly. Douglas McClary, first secretary of the British Show Racer Federation and author of an excellent book on how to show pigeons entitled *The Show Racer*, used to emphasise this by saying that an empty perch is often more valuable than a perch with a pigeon on it.

Some show fanciers allow their birds to fly out and exercise; others do not, and keep their birds in the lofts although they

119

provide enough room for the birds to exercise and stretch their wings sufficiently to keep them pliable. With the show season concentrated into so few weeks, the more active fanciers find that their preparation of birds continues from one show to another. Of course, some are more clever than others in maintaining birds in condition, just as some racing fanciers are especially good at conditioning their birds for races. Each individual fancier should work out for himself what is the best preparation for his birds.

However, once you have decided on your feed for the birds, try to keep to it, only adding the occasional titbit in your visits to the loft. Any sudden change of diet can be upsetting to the birds and lead to problems with their show condition. This was why, when manager of the British team for the Pigeon Olympiad, I always asked each owner for enough corn on which to feed his birds whilst they were in my care. One fancier, T.J. Davies of Llanelli, used to provide me with a packet for each of his birds for each day, with the ring number of the bird on each individual packet. Tommy's success in these competitions was quite outstanding (see Chapter 13), and I am sure it was in no small way due to such attention to detail. The subject of feeding is one on which ideas vary. There are successful fanciers in the show world who maintain that a diet of all beans is best. Only after birds return to their loft from a show, having perhaps been away for two or three days, do they vary this by giving a lighter feed — for example, seeds or oatmeal and rice — which can be digested with reasonable ease. This lighter feed is necessary because the journey to the show and the time in the pens, with so many people around, stresses the birds almost as much as a long-distance race. Racing fanciers who have tried their hand in classic shows will vouch for this.

It is very important that the birds are accustomed as far as possible to show conditions. By being brought from the loft in the basket and from there transferred to the pen, if possible extending the time spent in each until you have virtually reached show demands, your birds will gain experience and be as calm at their first show as if they had been going to such events for years. This will give them the advantage over untrained birds which can appear quite wild in the pen — something that judges do not like. In addition, birds that act wildly in the pen run the risk of damage to their flights and tails. It is essential that young birds for showing should be accustomed as early as possible to the pen and to the handling they will probably be subjected to from the judges. They should be carefully taken from their perches and gently placed in the show basket. Let them spend an hour or so in the basket, then place them in a show pen, but try to have an experienced old bird in the next pen so that they can see it standing quietly and happy in its surroundings. Have a show-pen drinker handy, place it between the two pens and quietly trickle a little water into it. The older bird will soon take a drink, and even if it does not do so on this first occasion the young bird will soon learn the secret. The same method can apply to feeding; the old bird will eat a titbit fed in the pen and the youngster will soon pick up the habit. Habit is the key word, for that is what the routine for shows should become.

Time spent training is time well spent, but it will be of little value unless you also show patience and devote time to your show entries at basketing before sending them or taking them to the show venue. Make sure the basket is quite clean, particularly when preparing for your first show of the season, for a basket stored away for any length of time will have accumulated dust which could be a source of mite-infection. Make sure each compartment of the basket is clean, that the partitions are sound and secure and that they have a good base of sawdust or woodchips, preferably the former for it seems to soak up droppings better and can prevent the soiling of feathers in transit.

When you put your birds in the basket, try to examine each as though you were the judge, and even if it is not your general practice to be super-critical, you should be on these occasions. Look for faults in them; do not become over-confident. It is only natural that a fancier should think his birds are the best,

121

in fact almost perfect; but in this mood you can very easily overlook faults.

Never rush the basketing of birds; they are better off spending a slightly longer time confined than being picked up in a rush and scrambled into a basket. In the same vein, give yourself plenty of time when arriving at shows, so that you can have a final check of the birds as you pen them. It does not pay to overhandle pigeons, but attention to little details like the straightening of an odd flight or the cleaning of dirty feet are all worthwhile. Pigeons which have an hour or two to become acclimatised to their new surroundings before judging will stand a greater chance than those penned at the very last moment. Remember, you are asking the birds to achieve success for you, so give them every consideration. Showing is a specialist game, and requires much concentration.

On return from a show, birds need to be allowed to settle again into their home surroundings and to return to their normal physical state and mental calm. If possible, their owner should be in the loft with them, the quiet tone of his voice and his gentle movements about the loft restoring their confidence.

Some Notable Shows

If you have decided to specialise in showing, you should join your local Show Racer society. The address is obtainable from the secretary of the British Show Racer Federation (see Appendix I).

The oldest of the main classic shows which take place during the show season is the Racing Pigeon Old Comrades Show which was first staged in 1928. It started as a reunion of those who had served with the Army Pigeon Services during World War I, and their commanding officer, Lt Col A.H. Osman, who was then editor of *The Racing Pigeon*, suggested that it should become an annual event. After the initial show a sum of around £5 was presented to the London Hospital and from then on, until the hospitals were nationalised, varying sums were donated to them. Since 1948 the show has been run annually in aid of the Royal Star and Garter Home for disabled sailors, soldiers and airmen at Richmond. It is generally held in the first weekend in December.

Incidentally, most of the major classic shows in Great Britain are run in aid of various charities. One of the first of the season is the Larkhill Pioneer Show in Scotland, usually held in the first week of October. Other outstanding shows are the Royal Pigeon Racing Association (RPRA) show at Blackpool, the Edinburgh International Charity Show, the Great Yorkshire Amalgamation at Harrogate, the Midland Show at Stoke, the Irish National Flying Club Show in Belfast, the RPRA's Southern Region Show at Basingstoke and the Welsh National Show. There are also many other smaller events.

That many of these shows present the proceeds to charities, emphasises the outstanding generosity of pigeon-racing fanciers. For at all times of the year, whenever a charitable cause arises on a local or national basis, fanciers seem to rally round to organise sales or shows to raise funds. It would be interesting if all these charitable efforts could be collated so that the sport's actual contribution to charities in one year could be known. A few years ago I tried to research this figure myself but lacked time to complete it; I had however reached a figure of approximately £200,000.

II
Officials and Organisations

So far we have talked mostly about the fancier's concern with his own birds and his own individual loft, but pigeon racing would not be possible if he looked no further afield than that. To be a good fancier one must take an interest in the various bodies set up to organise the sport and its administration.

The original body set up in Great Britain was the National Homing Union, now known as the Royal Pigeon Racing Association. It covers most of the country and is divided into twelve local regions. Particulars of these are given in Appendix I, and the local secretary will supply the newcomer to the sport with information concerning clubs within his region. The other racing bodies are the five Homing Unions: the Irish, North of England, North West, Scottish and Welsh (see Appendix I), which were formed as breakaways from the original body for the purpose of closer local administration. All racing-pigeon clubs are affiliated to one of these six bodies.

The basis of all successful organisation of the sport is, however, the individual fancier. Therefore, when you join your local club you should be prepared to listen to the club officers and also be willing to assist them in any way you can in the general running of the club. But, even if you are a young member, do not be afraid to ask if you are not sure why certain things are done. I know that when I was at the tender age of about ten my club officers must, at times, have been rather tired of my persistent questions; but they showed patience and answered them, and from these answers I gained the knowledge which has enabled me to carry out most of the official positions in the sport over many years. Remember that, although members of a club are competing against one another in races, they are all members of the team which makes up the club and that you can only take out of a club what you put in, so make every effort to create friendliness and companionship among your fellow members.

Never be afraid to voice your opinion at club meetings, but try not to be dogmatic; be prepared to listen to what other members say, and weigh up their views in the light of what would be best for the club as a whole. For this reason it may be better to broach some matters through the secretary in a quiet way rather than in an open meeting. For instance, if you think there has been an error in a club race result, I am sure he will be only too pleased to investigate the matter. You can be sure that if an error has been made it will not have been by design. We are all human and we can all make mistakes.

Club officers normally consist of a president, vice-presidents, chairman, secretary, treasurer, auditor(s) and committee. The last, in most small clubs, means all members; but for clubs with a particularly large membership or an extremely large area, a management committee may be selected to organise and carry out the club business. The president is generally an active member of the club, but in some clubs he is a sponsor or non-fancier who is interested in helping the organisation and, in appreciation of his help, the members invite him to be their figurehead. The same applies to vice-presidents. But usually both these types of officials are fanciers who have served the club in an exceptional manner or are long-standing members.

The chairman's duties are as his title implies: he is the person who normally occupies the chair at club or committee meetings. One of his most important functions is to familiarise himself with the rules of the organisation so that, if occasion arises, he can give guidance if requested on any matter concerning administration. In his capacity as chairman it is his duty to control the meeting in such a way that all present have the opportunity to express their views in a fair manner. He should study the rules of debate, make sure that only one person speaks at a time, and endeavour to see that no one person hogs the proceedings. At the end of a debate, before a motion is put to the vote, the chairman should, if he feels necessary, be prepared to sum up what has been said, but he should not emphasise his own personal opinion in doing so. This is not to say that the chairman, as a member, should be deprived of expressing his opinion in a debate; he can and should, at an opportune time in the discussion, express his views.

The treasurer's job is to see that the club's books and accounts are maintained in proper order and that the club's money is properly banked. He, with at least one other officer or committee member, should be signatories to cheques drawn on the club or society's bank account and, before signing any cheque, the treasurer should satisfy himself of the reason for payment.

In many racing-pigeon clubs the post of treasurer is combined with that of secretary, both being carried out by the same person. The secretary has probably the most important job in the organisation, but this knowledge should not lead him to think he is the boss — far from it. He is there as a responsible servant to the club or its committee, with the extreme responsibility of seeing that the committee's decisions are carried out. At all meetings he has the task of taking the minutes of the business transacted, and so needs to concentrate on all that is said and record the relevant details. As a member of the society or club, he can of course request the chairman's permission to speak on any subject if he feels he has a contribution to make. However, his paramount thought should be that he is the person responsible for seeing that the members' wishes are fulfilled, and that all necessary decisions of the committee are carried out.

The auditors may be members of the club or friendly outsiders. If they are internal people, they should not assume that their job is merely to check the club's annual balance sheet. They should interest themselves in the progress of the club's accounts throughout the year. No treasurer who is worth his salt would resent the request from the auditors for a spot check at any time; for he, like anyone else, is prone to error, and if one has been made it is better found sooner than later. If at any time the auditors feel things are not going right with the organisation financially, they should bring it to the attention of the committee so that matters can be put right as quickly as possible.

These then are the officials' duties as they apply to a local club; but basically they apply also to federations, combines and amalgamations, and even to the national bodies. Federations are generally convoying organisations formed to transport birds to the race points as inexpensively as possible. A group of clubs within a certain area get together and their birds are conveyed together, involving perhaps one or two people being employed to care for them *en route*, instead of one person for each club; at the same time they reap the benefits of shared conveyance. Birds used to be conveyed by rail, but unfortunately over the years British Rail has shown itself less and less interested in carrying livestock of any sort, and towards the end of the 1960s a large number of federations decided to switch to road transport and so became involved in purchasing their own vehicles in which to carry birds to race points.

The persons who accompany birds to the race points are known as 'convoyers', and these gentlemen have an extremely responsible job. In general, they are very keen fanciers, for their main task is to look after the welfare of the birds in transit and to see that, if the journey is to a long-distance race point, the birds are fed and given water on the journey. In addition, the convoyer often has the duty of obtaining special weather reports prepared by the Meteorological Office and, with his own knowledge of conditions as they exist at the race point and the advice of the Air Ministry as to the possible developments in the weather over the line of flight, makes up his mind whether to release the birds on a particular day or not. If he decides that the weather on the day scheduled for the race is too bad for the birds to have a fair chance, he will announce what fanciers refer to as a 'hold-over', and will see that the birds are well cared for and given food and drink. At the first opportunity he will despatch them on their flight home.

Sometimes, when the weather has deteriorated markedly and the forecast holds no prospect of improvement, the convoyer may decide to bring the birds home in their transporter. Better no race than a disaster or 'smash' that will leave many fanciers mourning the loss of their best birds — especially as the convoyer always receives the blame on such occasions.

Even with all this care, smashes do happen, and sometimes in the most propitious weather along the whole line of flight. The cause is unknown, though many years of research have gone into seeking the reason. The late Pierre Dordin, in particular, devoted his great experience to this study, and Tim Lovel's biography records his experiments and conclusions in detail.

In some organisations, obtaining the weather forecast is now done by the race adviser stationed at the home end of the course; but nevertheless the final decision on whether to liberate the birds rests with the convoyer. His is one of the most worrying and trying jobs in the sport of pigeon racing, for travelling to some race points may take as long as thirty-six hours; and although he may snatch some sleep, if he is a good convoyer, he is constantly thinking how best to look after the birds in his charge. But to such devoted fanciers, in spite of the considerable amount of work involved and the time spent away from home, it is an extremely rewarding, even pleasurable task.

Since federations are comprised of a group of clubs, it follows that every member is a club, and therefore the committee to carry out the administration of a federation must be comprised of representatives or delegates from those clubs. From those delegates the officers of the federation are elected. The federation committee generally decides on the race programme to be flown and this is adopted by the clubs. This does not mean that the individual club member has no say in where the races will be flown from — club members have the right to discuss any point concerning the federation at club meetings which are the forum to determine the wishes of the majority of members. Their delegates will be mandated to put these proposals to a federation meeting where they will be decided by a majority decision, and this democratic system applies to all matters covered by the federation.

Instructions to Stations at Which Homing Pigeons are Liberated.

Birds going in opposite directions must not be liberated within several minutes of each other or until the released birds have got clear away, otherwise large numbers of birds are diverted from their course and in the case of young untrained birds, many are lost by being carried off by birds flying a different course.

From the *Great Western Railway Appendix to the Service Time Tables*.

12
Disease and its Prevention

The prevention of disease is always better than cure. There is a tendency today for fanciers to become too involved with cures when they would do themselves and the Fancy as a whole far more good if they concerned themselves more with ways of prevention. Indeed, many fanciers never attempt to cure any ailing bird, but cull it at once.

Iodophors

A major breakthrough in disease prevention took place when iodophors were developed. Iodine had long been recognised as a bactericide and been used in various formulations as an antiseptic for minor wounds, in the sterilisation of instruments, etc, for purification of drinking water and as a prophylactic and therapeutic agent in diseases associated with bacteria, viruses and fungi. But there were serious limitations to its use — it is only slightly soluble in water, it stains and corrodes, and it is difficult to store due to its high vapour pressure. American researchers developed a tamed iodine which was water soluble, could be stored and did not stain or corrode as much as the original form. Once ways had been found to stabilise these iodophors, a new weapon was available to all involved with livestock and this, of course, includes the pigeon fancier.

Iodophors have proved to be excellent bactericides which not only inhibit but destroy many organisms including bacteria, viruses and fungi; and as such they are biocides rather than disinfectants. Modern formulations have exceptional wetting and penetrating, and sometimes detergent, properties, which enables cleaning and sterilisation to be accomplished in one operation. Most disinfectants are selective and, when purchasing, care must be taken to ensure that the product chosen will have the required action. This worry is removed if an iodophor such as Vykil is used. But make sure that whatever product is purchased it is 'Ministry Approved', meaning that it has been tested and found by the Ministry of Agriculture, Fisheries and Food (MAFF) to be effective against a wide variety of diseases. To date, pigeon fanciers do not appear to have appreciated the advantages that iodophors can bring.

To help prevent and control disease, transporters, panniers and all equipment should be treated with an iodophor. This will minimise the risks which are always present when large numbers of birds are brought into close contact. In the loft, fogging or spraying with an iodophor will guard against respiratory infections, paratyphoid and other bacterial infections, pigeon pox and other viral infections, aspergillosis and other fungal conditions. If fanciers would make use of such preventive measures, the disease problem would be far less acute. As a major step forward, fanciers should bring every pressure they can on their clubs and federations to ensure that communally used equipment is disinfected regularly.

Causes of Disease

It might be advantageous to consider what 'disease' really means. Disease is defined as a disorder of health, and 'health' as soundness of body. This means that any body disorder is a disease. Many people seem to refer to viral and bacterial infection as disease but think of worm infection, red-mite and other parasitic infection as something else. The latter may be easier to cure, but they are just as serious and must be prevented. But before examining ways of prevention, it may be helpful to list the causes of disease:

Bacteria: Paratyphoid, coryza, tuberculosis, one-eye cold, etc.
Protozoa: Canker.

131

Viruses: Pigeon pox, ornithosis, encephalomylitis, paramyxovir-
us, etc.
Fungi: Aspergillosis, thrush, etc.
Parasitic: Lice, fleas, mites, round- and hair-worm, etc.
Deficiency: Vitamin deficiency, mineral deficiency.

Bacterial diseases are mostly contracted by eating infected food, or come from stings, bites, wounds or inhalation. Viral diseases arise from infected drinking water, from a sneeze from another sick bird or other airborne contact. Fungus diseases are spread by wind, water or contact. Protozoa, such as the Trichomonas which causes canker, are often carried by parent birds without any symptoms and are passed to their youngsters by mouth.

Parasitic diseases are internal as the result of birds ingesting worms or their eggs, or external by contact with birds carrying on them some stage of parasite. It is essential that the fancier should have some understanding of the life-cycle of both types of parasite, because to control parasitic disease successfully this cycle must be broken. Much has been written on this subject and, thanks to the Medicine Act, the remedies available are effective and safe. As this chapter is concerned only with prevention we shall not detail any specific 'cures'.

Prevention

Mention of the risks present when many birds come together highlights the importance of ensuring that birds are not crowded into confined, badly ventilated spaces. The latter is a sure way of encouraging the spread of all types of diseases, even deficiency ones, as birds in such conditions will not feed readily or take the supplements provided to fortify their diet. Drinking water becomes contaminated, and the air stale, which provides a natural medium for the passage of infection. Parasitic infection is encouraged as food contaminated by droppings soon passes eggs, oocytes, etc, from one bird to another, and external parasites are passed by direct contact.

Lofts must be kept well ventilated and dry. A damp loft is

an ideal environment for many organisms causing disease. Fanciers should ensure that any floor-dressing they use is not simply cosmetic but has at least some bactericidal properties. To keep the loft free of external parasites such as lice, etc, a good brand of insecticide must be used on a regular basis. At least twice a year the loft should be treated with one of the residual (persistent) varieties to ensure the control of red-mite.

The need for the fancier to learn the life-cycle of parasites is shown by the following example: if one is treating an infestation of lice by spraying with an insecticide, it is essential to spray again after four weeks to ensure that the young lice, which have emerged since the birds were first sprayed, are effectively killed. For the eggs or nits are not killed by the spray, only the adult form. If this is not known, the initial treatment would be a waste of time as reinfestation would inevitably take place.

Adequate loft hygiene and routine treatment for worms, canker, coccidiosis and external parasites, together with the sensible use of minerals and vitamins, should be the aim of all fanciers. Such conduct would go a long way in the prevention of disease, and if such hygiene were extended to transporters and panniers on a national scale the incidence of disease would be almost minimal. Routine preventive treatment such as this is usually given before the breeding season starts, and again before the first race. Commonly used drugs for this purpose are amprolium for coccidiosis, aminonitrothiazole for canker (alias trichomoniasis), methyridine and/or piperazine for round-worm and pyrethrin for fleas and lice. Avoid poultry de-wormers such as mebendazole, which is toxic to pigeons when they are feeding youngsters. More controversial is the use of vaccine to prevent paramyxovirus — a variant of fowl pest or Newcastle disease — which has recently been reported in racing pigeons. It is claimed that this virus can be transmitted by pigeons back to domestic poultry, producing in them a mild form of fowl pest. At the time of writing, a programme of vaccination, using two doses of injected killed virus, is recommended by the RPRA and the MAFF, and is compulsory for all pigeons being raced to Britain from the Continent. The use of a live attenuated vaccine is prohibited in Britain, both for fear that it will mutate to a more virulent form and also because it is believed to be less effective. Many fanciers strongly dislike the vaccination programme. Others have agreed to it in order to protect their birds from this infection and in an attempt to obtain agreement for races from the Continent once again, after they were stopped in 1983.

Professional Help and Antibiotics

Provided the fancier is able to recognise symptoms, he needs simple basic knowledge rather than complicated technical terms, and there are ample medicines available to him. But unless he is certain that he has made the right diagnosis he must consult a veterinary surgeon to ascertain the real cause of the problem. With the ever-increasing value of birds, the cure of disease, if it does occur, may·be well worth the cost. Another factor which should be borne in mind when deciding whether or not to seek professional help, is that antibiotics should only be used on the advice of a veterinary surgeon. Their indiscriminate use as practised by some fanciers, if continued and increased, will be a source of danger not only to their own birds but also to the Fancy as a whole.

13
The International Scene

Pigeon racing is a worldwide sport enjoyed by fanciers in many countries. The international body, known as the Fédération Colombophile Internationale (see Appendix II), has its headquarters in Brussels and organises a congress every two years when delegates from the member countries meet to discuss the sport and any problems or proposals connected with it.

This international federation was first formed just prior to World War II and then, because of hostilities, was disbanded. However, it was re-formed in London in 1948 at the Racing Pigeon Old Comrades Show; the first post-war congress was held at Lille in 1949, and the event has been staged every two years since that date. In conjunction with the congress, an Olympiad is organised. As it is practically impossible to organise an event in which birds would race back to their own lofts from one starting point, a system has been devised whereby birds racing in competitions in their own countries qualify for entry into the Standard Class at the Olympiad, where the birds are judged to a very strict standard and points awarded to each bird.

Each country enters a team of ten — five cocks and five hens — and awards are made on both an individual and a team basis. The standard is set out by the international federation as shown in Fig 11. Judges have been known to part birds by one-hundredth part of a point, such is the strictness of the standard; however, generally they mark in multiples of one-quarter of a point. It seems that the Fédération Colombophile Internationale does not think there is a perfect pigeon, for although the allocation of points is based on 100, the instruc-

INTERNATIONAL JUDGING STANDARD

Pen No.   3501

MAX POINTS	POINTS JUDGED	POINTS AWARDED
10	HEAD, EYE and EXPRESSION	9.0
30	BALANCE and MUSCULATURE	28.5
15	GENERAL BONE STRUCTURE, BREAST BONE and NEAR FERCULA	14.0
15	BACK, BEGINNING OF TAIL and ITS ATTACHMENT TO BODY	13.0
30	WING and QUALITY OF FEATHERS	27.5
100	TOTAL ...	92.0

SIGNED

JUDGE

Fig 11   The International Judging Standard award card as presented by the author and Tony Cornwell when selecting birds for the British Olympiad teams

tion to judges at the Olympiad is that the highest mark awarded should be 93 and the lowest 85.

In the Standard Class team of five cocks and five hens, the cocks must have flown a total distance of 2,000km (1,243 miles). You can only count the races (for your 2,000km) that are 200km (124 miles) or over and have more than 100 pigeons competing, and your bird must be in the first 20 per cent of the positions. The only difference for the hens is that the total distance is 1,600km (994 miles).

When the pigeons are placed in the showing pens, their metal identity ring will be covered by a plastic cover so that the judges will not know what country a bird is from. Each judge in turn, and out of hearing of the judge who goes before or comes after, marks each pigeon on the International Standard Point system — the aforementioned 100. This number is broken down to cover the anatomy of the pigeon. At one time a set of notes was issued to assist the judges, and the following is a summary with the points allocation.

International Standard Class Judging

Head, Eye, Expression
A maximum of 10 points can be given for these. Unfortunately, the racing pigeon in strange surroundings will not always show itself to best advantage. It is by nature a nervous bird, so the judge must try to put it at ease, but attentive; if he cannot do this, it should not constitute a serious fault when scoring.

The pigeon is removed from the pen, and its head and eye examined. The head should be convex, completely rounded, not slightly flattened at the top. If it is a cock, the head should be bold and noble, the forehead having as much width as height. In the hen bird, the head is usually smaller and more recessed, giving a sweet look. The beak should be in proportion to the head and well formed. The wattle or nose should be dry and white and not over-developed, although age should be taken into account for some older cocks do show a bigger wattle than younger ones. The eye should be well set and shine with a lively glint, generally reflecting the health of the pigeon. The actual colour of the eye is not important, but the colour should be strong and not washed out.

Generally speaking, though no doubt there are exceptions, in good racing pigeons the eye is set a little forward and high in the head, so that if you pencilled a straight line from the slit of the beak across the pigeon's face, most of the eye would be above the line. The neck should not be swan-like and should be in good proportion to a firm pair of shoulders that denote power.

Balance and Muscle Structure
Balance and muscle structure carry a maximum of 30 points.

Here, a competitor can greatly assist his candidate by planning the time he feeds the pigeon before the judging takes place to ensure that the bird has removed any surplus food from its crop. It should sit erect when held in the hand and not drop forward. The body as a whole should be very firm and of an aerodynamic shape.

One should be able to feel supple muscles proportional to the pigeon's shape, and not covered with excess fat. The shoulders should be broad and should narrow off to give the appearance of compact wholeness with the beginning of the tail.

General Bone Structure

A maximum of 15 points can be given for general bone structure, including the breastbone or keel and the rear fork or vent. When one is feeling out the frame of the pigeon one also notices its weight; experience has proved that very few heavy pigeons win races, whatever the distance, whereas a great many small and light birds do. But it is the medium or medium-to-small that have the most winners in their ranks, and when you handle these pigeons they seem to rise in your hands, giving the impression of weightlessness.

Even so, the bone structure must be good and not show any deformities; the fork or vent must be tight. Of course one must be a little lenient with the hen pigeon for her pelvic bones have to part to allow the laying of eggs, but even so, the fork should be strong and not wide open and soft.

Back, Tail and Attachment of Tail to Body

These features can be awarded a maximum of 15 points. The alignment of the back should continue harmoniously in line through to the tail, which should be in proportion to the remainder of the bone structure — not too long or too short. When you hold the pigeon in two hands and run the thumbs (exerting very little pressure) down the back to the position where the tail flights begin, the tail should not protrude up into the air at a 45 degree angle, but should dip slightly.

138

Wing and Quality of the Plumage

Lastly, 30 points maximum can be awarded to wing and quality of plumage. Dealing with plumage first, the colour is not important but it should be strong and not fading. The feathers should be plentiful and silky in texture.

The wing is possibly the most controversial of all parts of a pigeon to judge, and many arguments have been provoked by this part of the pigeon's anatomy. The Colombophile Internationale Technical Committee says the arm of the wing should be thick, short and very strongly feathered, its attachment to the body the shortest possible, and it should be extremely supple. The wings themselves, when open, should be slightly incurved and supple. The secondary wing should be composed of feathers as wide as possible, and its length should be proportionate to the primary wing — from the inside secondaries the length of the flight should form a gentle curve when the wing is extended.

The four leading to outside flights of the primary wing should be ventilated so as to facilitate flying. The length of the wings should be in proportion to the body — about 20mm (¾in) short of the tail when the wings are at rest. They should not be too wide at the base and should be narrower and slightly rounded at the tip.

The smaller feathers covering the wing should be abundant, those on the top covering each other like tiles on a roof and extending as far as possible towards the back edges of the primary and secondary wings so as to strengthen them. The smaller feathers underneath the wing should be plentiful and silky to facilitate the flow of air during flight.

Winning Countries at the Olympiads

It was not until 1961 that a team from Great Britain was entered in the Olympiad which that year was held in Essen, West Germany. Made up of birds from all over Britain nominated and selected through *The Racing Pigeon* at the Old Comrades Show in London, this team took sixth place, and a Red Chequer hen owned by the late Trevor Parker — a Welsh miner from Treherbert — was awarded the highest number of points, 93, and adjudged the best bird in the Olympiad. This success for Trevor's pigeon, named Molly after his wife, started a considerable run of successes for British pigeons in the two-yearly competition. The winning team at Essen came from Belgium.

Two years later the event was staged in Ostend and the British team moved up into third place behind Czechoslovakia and Belgium. In the individual placings there was a dead-heat for best in show, with a Blue Chequer hen owned by L. Chitil of Czechoslovakia achieving the same number of points as a Blue Cock owned by Trevor Parker and named Olympic Vision. This bird was so named because, when the final selection for the British team was made by Tony Cornwell from Birmingham and Col A.H. Hopas from Sunderland, Col Hopas declared, 'There will not be a cock in Brussels to beat this one'. Trevor said he had to name the pigeon in appreciation of the colonel's vision.

The 1965 Olympiad and Congress was staged at Alexandra Palace in North London, when my colleague Colin Osman was appointed as organiser and I was his deputy. It was a great experience, and also a lesson, to witness all the hard work which goes into organising such an event. Entries were received from fourteen countries, and once again there was a close result between Czechoslovakia and Great Britain with a Dark Chequer hen owned by L. Bohumil of Czechoslovakia just shading a Red Chequer cock owned by Edgar Griffiths of Llanelli, South Wales, by a quarter of a point, to win the award of best in show. The team result went to Great Britain with Czechoslovakia second, followed by Belgium, Holland and France.

Two years later fanciers flocked to the beautiful Austrian

Pages 141–3 illustrate the twelve birds which comprised the Great Britain team for the 1983 Pigeon Olympiad in Prague. All photographs by Anthony Bolton.

(*top left*) Red Chequer Hen GB 78V 51458 owned by L. Rick; (*top right*) Blue White Flight Cock GB 78N 20126 owned by Paul Smith; (*bottom left*) Blue Hen GB 78N 27081 owned by Mr & Mrs P. Moss and Son; (*bottom right*) Dark Chequer Hen WHU 80H 3691 owned by H. Webley

(*top left*) Cheque Hen GB 76K 32004 owned by T. Haddock; (*top right*) Dark Chequer Pied Cock GB 79S 13730 owned by Swann & Lane; (*bottom left*) Blue Hen GB 76X 32004 owned by R. Newstead; (*bottom right*) Mealy Cock GB 80V 28321 owned by N. Nelmes

(*top left*) Blue Hen WHU 80H 6637 owned by Mr & Mrs Bridle & Son; Red Chequer Cock GB 79L 94940 owned by H. Weble; (*bottom left*) Red Chequer Cock GB 78N 20277 owned by Paul Smith; (*bottom right*) Blue Cock GB 79L 35034 owned by Mr & Mrs Ruffell and Son

143

capital, Vienna, for the Olympiad and Congress, with representatives of over twenty countries attending and teams of birds from sixteen countries. The Olympiad was somewhat swamped by the Great Britain team with the five hens taking first, second, third and joint fourth positions, and three of the five cocks taking second, third and fourth. The best bird award, however, escaped them, being won by a Blue cock owned by L. Bertreaux of France, although the best hen was owned by T.J. Davies of Llanelli. The team result featured the same five countries as in 1965: first Great Britain, second Czechoslovakia, third Holland, fourth France and fifth Belgium.

Katowice in Poland was the venue for 1969 and the event proved a double for Don Cardwell of South Wales who won the award for both best cock and best hen. The team result was first Holland, second Great Britain and third Czechoslovakia. In Brussels two years later the best hen was owned by Mr and Mrs Pugh of London; and in Düsseldorf in 1973 the award for the best cock went to T.J. Davies. Success continued, with the team taking third place in Budapest in 1975 and second to West Germany when the event was staged in Blackpool in 1977.

In 1978 the Ministry of Agriculture and Fisheries instituted a regulation that pigeons imported into this country had to undergo thirty-five days in quarantine, with the result that British fanciers were reluctant to enter their best birds for international competitions, because on their return they were regarded as imports and subject to the conditions laid down by the ministry. Thus performance went down, with the team taking only seventh place in Amsterdam in 1979, eleventh in Tokyo in 1981, and seventeenth in Prague in 1983. The winning teams in those years were Czechoslovakia in 1979 and 1983, and Holland in 1981.

International Races
For about the last fifteen years several Continental countries have joined together in the organisation of international races,

and birds from Belgium, Holland, Luxembourg, France and West Germany have competed annually in races from places such as Pau, just on the French side of the Pyrenees; Barcelona in Spain; and Narbonne, Marseilles and Perpignan, all in France. In most of these events the Belgian or West German birds have been among the leaders. British fanciers did not compete in these events for years, although the London Columbarian Society under its fine secretary, the late Frank Kightly, organised an open event for British fanciers which was flown from Barcelona in conjunction with the international event. Some good performances were recorded over the years, notably by Pinney Brothers of Yeovil who recorded the first pigeons into Britain in two consecutive years in this London Columbarian open event; their good Dark Chequer cock was 2nd in 1956, 3rd in 1957 and 1st in 1958.

From about 1975 onwards interest among British fanciers in these international events increased, and an organisation known as the British International Championship Club was formed to compete in them. This gave rise to some really fine performances, notably from a hen owned by Bill Cushley of Bristol named Bel Avon which was the first bird into Britain in the British International Championship from Pau in 1975, second from Pau in 1976 and tenth in the same organisation's Pau race in 1977 (not to be confused with the National Flying Club event from the same point). In 1975 the same bird was thirty-first Open in the event from around 4,000 entries. Hopes were high for a British win in 1983 but alas, an outbreak of disease on the Continent led to a complete ban on racing from Europe.

14
High-flying
and Exhibition Varieties

A large number of fanciers keep pigeons other than racing pigeons. Broadly, these birds fall into two categories: the high-flying types which appeal to those who like to see their birds flying around their home, and the show or exhibition types which do not fly outside the loft and which are ornamental rather than practical. Usually the fanciers who keep these pigeons are members of the National Pigeon Association (see Appendix I) which publishes an official journal and from whom the addresses of clubs or societies specialising in particular breeds can be obtained. These clubs organise shows, exhibitions and competitions.

Pigeon societies were known over 250 years ago and the first English society, believed to have been founded around 1720, organised shows of Carrier Pigeons, Pouters and Tumblers. It was about 150 years later that the first shows were staged in the United States of America. Over the years so many breeds of these non-racing pigeons have evolved that it is impossible to mention them all. It must be remembered that their history is very ancient; it was after all the dove, so closely related, that as Noah's messenger returned to the ark with the olive branch.

One thing that the fancy breeds have in common with the racing pigeon is that in most cases their lofts are very similar. For the breeds which do not go out to fly in the air, however, an aviary is built on so that the birds can spend time in the sunshine on good days.

The training of pigeons to fly high was once a very popular sport, but it declined when fanciers began to send birds to race long distances rather than circle round one point. In Great Britain the main high-flying pigeons are the Flying Tippler, the Birmingham Roller, and the West of England Tumbler. Flying Tipplers are pedigree birds and, if you wish to obtain birds which will fly for any length of time, they should be descended from known good-performance strains.

The activities of fanciers who keep Flying Tipplers are akin to those of the racing-pigeon man, for flying competitions are based on endurance and stamina. The birds are trained to fly for very long hours but, except for the first hour, they must remain in sight of their lofts. Flights of over fourteen hours have been recorded with young birds, and between eighteen and twenty hours with old birds. The birds are liberated at their lofts by their owners in the presence of an independent referee, and are then allowed to fly continuously until their owner puts out his droppers, or decoy birds, to induce them to drop on to the loft. The whole of the team must drop and enter the loft within one hour of the droppers being put out. The competition team is usually five birds, but must be at least three.

The Birmingham Roller, as the name suggests, originated in the industrial West Midlands where workers, after being confined in factories for long hours, gained great pleasure from watching their birds perform in the sky. The Roller generally weighs about 7oz (198g), approximately half the weight of a racing pigeon. In flight it can turn over five times in a second, dropping 5ft (1.5m) whilst tumbling; thus speed is all-important. After rolling, the birds level out in flight, climb a little, and then enjoy another series of rolls. It is thrilling to watch a team of Birmingham Rollers at exercise; they normally fly for something over half an hour.

The West of England Tumbler has an abundance of good silky feathering and is mainly white in colour — in fact most judges insist on all the wing flights being white if this bird is to be considered at exhibition. Many fanciers today only keep this breed for exhibition, and do not let their birds out. Unlike the Birmingham Roller, when they spin in the air West of

England Tumblers do not lose height, but perform one quick spin and then rejoin the rest of the flock.

Other notable flying breeds are the Danzig High Flyer, the Orlik and the pure white Cumulet. The last mentioned originated in France and was introduced into Britain towards the end of the nineteenth century; but with the spread of long-distance pigeon racing it became almost extinct and in Britain today is included for exhibition purposes in the 'Any Other Variety' class. The Danzig High Flyer is, as the name implies, an expert on really high soaring flight for long periods, usually alone. It has a crest on the back of the head, and a very full tail, almost like that of a fantail. It occurs in all colours.

The Orlik, meaning in Polish a young eagle, is unique in flying with the tail fanned, gliding round as thermal currents lift it higher. Its secondary flight feathers are longer than usual, and these, together with the fanned tail, give an appearance of a flying semicircle as it circles. In colour the Orlik is a deep red with a little white in the tail and sometimes in the wing tips. One other breed of the Roller group — the Oriental Roller which, as its name suggests, originated in Far Eastern countries — was introduced into Great Britain during the nineteenth century, probably by Turkish traders. Its rather long tail has sixteen to eighteen feathers compared with the twelve of other breeds. It flies swiftly for short periods.

Varieties of the Tumbler family are also generally kept for exhibition; in Britain there are two types — the Short-faced and the Long-faced. It has been said that the Short-faced Tumbler was created by artificial means, in that the heads or skulls were tampered with before the bones had really set by being depressed by a wooden instrument pressed into the bottom of the forehead almost daily. It has also been alleged that there were many fatal results due to this cruel procedure. But this is unlikely to be true, for according to Darwin any physical characteristic acquired after birth cannot be transmitted to the young. It is far more likely that a short-faced pigeon occurred naturally by mutation, and clever fanciers 'fixed' it by the inbreeding techniques already described. A disadvantage of the short-faced breeds of pigeon is that the parents cannot feed their own young after they are about a week old, because the mandibles of adult and chick cannot grip together properly. The young have therefore to be fostered out to others with normal beaks. The short-faced adult can, however, feed the young of the foster parents, if desired.

The Long-faced Tumbler has a much bolder crown to the head which is much broader across the front. The head appears quite rounded and the eye seems set far more centrally in the head than in the short-faced bird. Colourings and markings in both birds are rather similar, although the short-faced variety generally carries the wings below the tail, whilst in the Long-faced Tumbler they are usually set above the tail.

Several types of pigeon are noted for their tendency to display themselves in the exhibition pen. One, the Fantail, is very attractive when it displays; as the name indicates, its tail is like a fan. The cultivation of this breed over the years has led to the tail containing many more feathers than is normal in a pigeon. The number varies considerably, the average being between thirty and thirty-two, but forty-two has been recorded. The breed is believed to have originated in the Orient, probably in India or China.

Fantails, when displaying, lean the head right back against the tail, the breast becomes almost oval shaped and sometimes the head becomes almost invisible. One particularly beautiful variety of this breed is the Lace Fantail, so named because the tail feathers are so thin that when the tail is opened and displayed it looks like a piece of finely woven lace.

Another group of bird, including the Croppers and Pouters, display by blowing out the crop. Actually the phrase is a little misleading; it is the filling of the air sacs surrounding the crop which gives the balloon-like appearance. Owing to the large size of the crop of these birds, breeders usually use foster parents for the rearing of young birds. Racing pigeons of medium size are regarded as the best for this.

The adult birds are quite long-legged, so that show-cages used for exhibiting these are dome-shaped, and the bird is usually provided with a square block of wood on which to stand when blowing. These birds do not seem particularly popular, and I have seen very few when visiting exhibitions of fancy birds. The standard English Pouter originated in the eighteenth century, and stands 16–20in (40–50cm) high. With its long feathered legs, dignified stance and inflated chest, a good bird looks most impressive.

The Pigmy Pouter is a smaller version, and the Norwich Cropper is intermediate in size between them, but has a much larger crop. These, too, need feeders to bring up their young. The Holle Cropper goes back to the sixteenth century and is the most popular 'blowing' breed. Other old breeds in this group, such as the Dutch and German Croppers, are rarely seen today.

The Modena breed of pigeon is popular for shows. They are bred in varying colours, and a particular feature is that the bars can be in contrasting colours with, for instance, a blue pigeon carrying distinctly red bars. As the name indicates, this pigeon originated in Italy; it was at first used for flying competitions but is now kept solely for exhibition.

A very pretty exhibition pigeon is the Satinette with, as its name implies, feathers looking rather like satin; these birds are mainly white in colour, but have coloured coverts and tail feathers. They have heavily feathered legs, and usually grow a pronounced frill on the breast.

15
The Year in the Loft

In keeping pigeons, as in most other activities, the seeds of success or failure are sown many months before their harvest is gathered. By the time the races are being started, therefore, the wise fancier has made all his preparations, and is reasonably confident of the outcome. Of course, unpredictable factors such as strong winds may rob him of success — or occasionally may help him — and an element of luck can always influence the outcome. But there is only a little that a fancier can do in June or July to help his birds; the real work is done in the preceding months and years.

The pigeon-fancier's year may be said to start in the autumn when the races are over and the birds go into heavy moult; it is then that the new feathers for the next season's racing are grown and it is vitally important that these should be as strong and supple as possible. Damaged feathers will give way under stress, and this is particularly so if fretmarks are allowed to appear due to faulty nutrition. This is not the time to neglect the birds or keep them short of rations. The aim should not be to overfeed, for this will lay down unwanted surplus body fat; but a good nutritious mixture with plenty of protein for further growth is essential. It is no surprise to find that of the various commercial mixtures of grains and seeds marketed in Belgium, the one that contains the most different kinds of seed is the Moulting Mixture. Good feeding is particularly needed by young birds which have to grow their permanent feathers and are also putting on bone and muscle as they mature. Faulty feeding at this stage will assuredly cause them to be a disappointment in the following season.

As the autumn days shorten, the fancier gradually introduces his winter regime; the birds are kept quiet, and under bad weather conditions they should not go out. This is particularly so if there is really heavy rain, fog or falling snow. Under these conditions there is no advantage in letting them out, and everything to be lost. But heavy frosts or a carpet of snow need not make any difference, and the birds seem to revel in these cold but bright conditions. Some fanciers, however, never let their birds out for the whole winter, and this is particularly the case if predacity from hawks or cats is a problem in their area. Other fanciers go to work before dawn and return after dusk so that flights during the working week are impossible unless a member of their family helps them. At all times the aim should be to avoid the birds putting on excess fat, thus preserving good muscle tone and buoyant health.

Clearly, when it is cold the birds will need more food and they will want less when it is mild. Many fanciers give a feed containing as much as 30 to 40 per cent barley when the birds come in from a flight. This grain is nutritious but the birds do not really like the taste of it, so that they will only eat what hunger dictates and as soon as their appetite is satisfied they will leave the surplus.

Now is the time when the fancier will make any essential alterations to his loft. Even quite trivial changes may disrupt the birds in their normal daily life, and if this work is done in the middle of the racing season the outcome can be disastrous. Far better to make notes in a diary or day book during the summer and then in autumn and winter put the ideas into practice. The birds then have ample time to get used to the alterations.

It is also the time when the stock of birds left at the end of the racing season should be critically reviewed. Did each of them give a satisfactory performance? Is there a danger of being overstocked? Are the birds past their best or can they give one more season's racing? Alternatively should they be retired to stock to produce young birds for the future? Only the fancier, aided once again by his invaluable records, can come to a conclusion whether a bird should be kept or culled.

Some birds take time to mature, especially those of strains such as the Dordin which have very big frames and should never be finally judged wanting until their second or even third racing season. Above all one should avoid being over-stocked because of the problem of disease and the impossibility of knowing each bird individually if it is just one of a large crowd. Often the most successful racing lofts are those which seem almost empty when you enter them.

Again winter is the time when introduction of new stock should be considered. If the fancier decides that an out-cross should be brought in to strengthen a point in his own birds that he finds less than satisfactory, this is the time to do it; and it is essential to give a great deal of thought to the matter. Particularly if a family is rather closely in-bred, even if it is winning well, now is the time to try an out-cross, the aim being to find a bloodline that will succeed or 'nick' with one's own. The young birds from such a cross must be tested thoroughly by racing and, if successful, cautiously mixed with the fancier's old family. It is essential to choose a strain that is as good as, if not better than, your own; and if one has to decide that the existing loft of pigeons is giving no satisfaction at all, it is better to bring in one or two birds, not to cross with the duffers, but to pair together. Their eggs can then be farmed out to the other birds which are used only as feeders and the new strain can be rapidly multiplied.

Characteristics sought to improve a strain may include such items as silky feathers, a particularly strong bone structure, persistence in getting home in bad weather, or more fire and dash, especially if sprint races are the aim. In the latter case an out-cross should not be brought in from a loft where there are just one or two famous star pigeons, but from a loft where the whole team of young birds — and the yearlings, two-, three- and four-year-olds — win their races in convincing style.

The winter months are also the time to decide on the pairing of your birds and, as already mentioned, many happy hours can be spent both in the warmth of one's own house and in the loft making decisions on paper. The fancier himself must decide whether to inbreed quite closely, or to keep the relationship as distant as possible within a strain, or to cross two or three strains to seek hybrid vigour (see Chapter 4). He also has to decide when to pair up. The most usual time is mid-February, which means that the older birds are ready for the early races that begin around the end of April. However, those fanciers who are aiming for the longer-distance races which occur in late June and July, will probably defer pairing up until the middle of March. On the other hand some fanciers want a team of strong, active young birds as early as possible in the year, either to give them the best hope for success in young-bird racing or so that they can sell the first clutches hatched to other fanciers. These people will pair their birds up in mid-December so that they can have their young birds ready for ringing as soon as the new season's rings are issued.

If this is done, special precautions need to be taken to ensure that good-quality youngsters are raised. It is essential that the loft is warm enough to prevent the drinking water freezing, for pigeons must always have access to water when they feed. Artificial light in the loft is helpful, both to prolong the day so that the young birds can be fed for longer and also so that attention can be given in the morning before work or in the evening after the fancier returns. If light is provided, a dimmer switch is essential to allow the birds time to get back on to their nests before the light goes out. Extra supplies of cod-liver oil are helpful in the winter because there is no sunshine to manufacture Vitamin D naturally and this vitamin is essential for good bone formation. Extra nesting material such as straw or hay may help to keep the young birds warm and, as soon as they have been ringed, be prepared to exchange them around between the nests so that the two youngsters in any one nest are always of equal size. This is because it often happens that the first hatched pigeon is so much stronger than its brother or sister that it outstrips it in size and in its demand for food. It should not be assumed that the smaller one will catch up — far from it; for in fact the

Young birds grow rapidly: from left to right, 3 days, 7 days and 12 days old

difference will steadily increase. Far better to swap it for the bigger one from another pair of youngsters so that the two large birds can grow together and the two smaller ones can compete on equal terms for their parents' attention.

The rearing of good young birds does not happen by chance, and only attention to the smallest detail will produce the finest youngsters. There is all the difference in the world between a young bird that on weaning is plump almost to the point of fatness, has copious silky plumage and sits quietly in its nest-box content with the world, and a scrawny, puny young bird that is always whining for food, light in the hand, bony, inadequately feathered and already a prey to the many diseases that lie in wait for it. Again, don't imagine that the scrawny youngster will 'catch up' or 'make one on the day'. It never will, and furthermore it will spread its diseases and worms among the rest of your young-bird flock. Far better to

155

Two squeakers who are the same age but from different parents: on the left a thin scrawny hungry bird always squeaking for food; on the right a contented plump well-feathered youngster. Inferior young birds are not worth keeping

give it a quick tap on the head the moment you realise that it is of low standard. The whole of pigeon racing is devoted to achieving the highest possible standard in one's birds, because only then can one hope to beat those of the many other fanciers; the slightest weakness, imperfection or departure from good health is sufficient to doom the enterprise before it starts.

The decision whether to fly on the Natural or on the Widowhood System will have been taken long before the beginning of the races, for the whole campaign, and indeed the structure of the loft, is different. Years ago it used to be normal in this country to fly the Natural System, but gradually the Widowhood System gained the upper hand, first in Belgium where Renier Gurnay first made it popular, and in the last ten years it has gained ground in Britain too. The great

156

advantage of the system is not that the birds fly faster, but that they leave the point of release, and trap when they return home, quicker on average than the Natural birds do. Another considerable advantage is that the nest position does not alter, because no eggs are incubated or chicks fed. The same birds can be raced week after week or, in the longer races, at least fortnightly. However, if some of them become stale and blasé, the wise fancier realises that the mere reward of seeing the hen for a few minutes or even an hour or two after each race is not enough for the cock.

At this point it is sometimes necessary to let a Widowhood cock and his hen build a new nest, and lay a new clutch of eggs in order to rekindle the vital spark and the will to fly home as quickly as possible. This is difficult, because it removes that cock from racing for approximately three weeks and also unsettles all the other cocks when they see one of their number settling down to domestic bliss while they are still deprived of their mates. It is therefore sometimes essential to remove such a pair to another loft, if possible identical in all respects to their previous one, even to the point of having their nest-box in exactly the same position. There they can sit on the eggs for 10–12 days, have three weeks' rest and then go back on to the Widowhood System as before. Tricks such as these distinguish the successful fancier from the average. They are less important in very long-distance races where the quality of the birds themselves can make up for deficiencies in the fancier, but in the middle and particularly sprint distances, management is the key to success.

The popularity of the Widowhood System does not, however, mean that Natural flying is completely outmoded; in fact many of our successful fanciers still use this method exclusively. But under this system a more careful check has to be kept on the precise status of each individual bird. For instance, it is risking disaster to send an excited cock, particularly a yearling, either to be trained or to fly a race when it is ardently driving its hen to lay; though exceptionally, some very good winning times have been recorded in just such a nest situation. But in general it is a risky time, and many yearlings are so excitable that they forget all the careful training that has been instilled into them and career madly all over the countryside, becoming hopelessly lost. Similarly a hen should never be sent to a race when just about to lay an egg; she cannot do herself justice and indeed may refuse to fly at all if she feels the egg is imminent. But apart from these provisos, as mentioned in Chapter 7, birds differ widely as to the best time for them to fly. Once such a winning situation has been found, however, one can be fairly confident that the same will be good for that bird next year. This is particularly true of hens.

One of the most successful Belgian fanciers, Raymond Cobut, has specialised extremely successfully in preparing hens for long-distance races. In his experience hens are particularly good for these great distances, particularly the two-day events; they will fly longer into the dusk before settling and at first light they are up and off again. This is an enormous advantage over the Widowhood cocks that will settle earlier, and in the morning will take longer to preen and perhaps search for a drink before resuming their flight. Cobut's preparation is meticulous — a special loft compartment is used for the hens that are to fly in these races, and usually the birds are prepared with only one race in mind. Their mates do not fly at all, for it has been found by bitter experience that it is impossible for both to do justice; and if there is a hold-over, or if one of the pair is lost, then the nest is ruined and everything has to be started again.

The hens are usually paired up in mid-March and are allowed to sit and to rear one youngster. They then lay again and the eggs are carefully moved around so that the hen is sitting or feeding a chick at exactly the stage she flies best at when the race takes place. Feeding for these hens is the same as for cocks — a light mixture in the morning and a more ample one with more protein in the evening. They have one or two unforced flights a day and are slowly brought on until, as yearlings, they will fly perhaps 400km (249 miles), as two-year-olds 600km (373 miles) and at between three and six years old the really long-distance races.

As the racing season progresses, the fancier's thoughts turn to his young birds which are being weaned and each evening going out on to the top of their loft; for in these birds rest all his hopes for the future. At first they enjoy just going out on to their loft top; soon the more adventurous ones are taking small flights by themselves, tumbling and swooping in a carefree way that looks certain to end in disaster. Yet it is surprising how very seldom a youngster comes to grief in these aerobatics. Before long they start to bunch together as a flock or kit that circles round and round overhead, and then on one heart-stopping day they are suddenly gone. This 'ranging' as it is called, is a perfectly normal happening. From time to time the fancier will see them sweep across the sky as though they are reassuring themselves that their loft is still there, and then they are gone again for perhaps fifteen or twenty minutes. Sometimes they are gone for an hour or more and then suddenly are circling overhead once more. Often they go to a tremendous height, especially in very clear bright cloudless weather. Remember what has been said — that it is vital to avoid their being picked up by a race team and carried off many miles to become totally lost. Stick to evening, not weekend, exercise during the racing season; for by evening most races are over and any birds crossing will be in ones and twos that do not exert the same fatal magnetism as a big flock of several hundred.

When the young birds are ranging freely every evening, it is time to begin their training. This must be thoroughly and patiently done, for without it young birds never mature into dependable adults. As yearlings they may look magnificent, may train excellently and even fly well once or twice; but when the going is hard or they have to make most of the journey on their own they will become hopelessly lost and very often never be seen again if they do not have thorough grounding as young birds in the art of returning home as quickly and as directly as possible. This cannot be too strongly emphasised, for without adequate young-bird training — which comes inconveniently near the summer holidays, clashes with the

159

Nest-box Home for each pair of birds provided within the loft.

Overfly Difference in distance between two lofts when one is further from the race point than the other.

Plumage General feathering.

Primaries The ten flight feathers furthest from the body.

Race point Starting place of pigeon race.

Ringer Machine used for placing rubber ring on pigeon's leg for racing.

Rubber Specially printed marked rubber ring placed on bird's leg when entered for a race.

Secondaries The flight feathers nearer the body.

Settle Acclimatise birds to new loft or environment.

Squeaker Young bird in nest.

Toss Usually refers to liberating birds from short distances, eg a 48km (30 mile) toss is a training flight from that distance.

Training Taking birds short distances from home to fly back.

Velocity Average speed of pigeon in a race expressed in metres (yards) per minute.

Vent The combined opening (cloaca) for excretion from the intestine and kidneys and for laying eggs.

Wattle The white fleshy tissue at the base of a pigeon's beak.

Appendix I
Addresses in the United Kingdom

Royal Pigeon Racing Association (RPRA): General Manager, Major L. Lewis, MBE, The Reddings, Nr Cheltenham, Gloucestershire, GL51 6RN (Telephone 0452 713529)

Regional Secretaries of the RPRA

Cumbria (whole of Cumbria): D. Singleton, 57 Foundry Street, Barrow-in-Furness, Cumbria, LA14 2BB (0229 27777)

Derbyshire and South Yorkshire: L. Henshaw, 4 Green Lane, Askern, Doncaster, DN6 OPX (0302 700440)

Devon and Cornwall: T.R. Mallett, Locarno, St Nicholas Street, Bodmin, Cornwall (0208 3016)

East Midland (Beds, Cambs, Leics, Lincs, Norfolk, Northants, Notts, Suffolk): R.S. Linley, 'Conray', Middlewood Green, Earl Stonham, Stowmarket, Suffolk (044 971383)

Irish: L. Boyle, 3 Greedyke Walk, Dromore, County Down, Northern Ireland (0846 692102)

London: M.V. Farrant, 133 Dennett Road, Croydon, Surrey (01-684-3583)

North East (Cleveland, Durham, Humberside, Northumberland, Tyne and Wear, N Yorks, W Yorks): D.K. Higgins, 6 Billingwood Drive, Rawdon, Leeds (0532 504810)

North West (Greater Manchester, Lancs): J.B. Newson, 20 Gorsey Lane, Banks, Southport, Merseyside (0704 224017)

Southern (Berks, Bucks, Hants, Isle of Wight, Oxfordshire, Surrey, E Sussex, W Sussex): W.J. Chapman, 26 Bamburgh Close, Reading, Berks, RG2 7UD (0734 84255)

South Western (Avon, Dorset, Glos, Somerset, Wilts): F. Burton, 30 Meadow Road, Charlton Marshall, Blandford, Dorset (0258 2063)

163

Welsh (Dyfed, Gwent, Mid Glam, S Glam, Powys): W. Jones, 44 Excelsior Street, Waunlwyd, Ebbw Vale, Gwent

Western (Cheshire, Clwyd, Gwynedd, Merseyside, Salop): Miss B.M. Stretton, Whitegates, Lilleshall, Newport, Salop (0952 603279)

West Midland: J.G. Edwards, 276 Dawlish Road, Selly Oak, Birmingham, 29 7AU (021 472 3846)

Secretaries of the Homing Unions

Irish Homing Union: K. McConachie, 38 Ballynahatty Road, Belfast, BT8 8L3

North of England Homing Union: A. Rothwell, 58 Ennerdale Road, Walker Dene, Newcastle-upon-Tyne, NE6 4DG (0632 625440)

North West Homing Union: K. Borrowdale, 37 Tarn Road, Thornton, Blackpool, FY5 5AY (0253 823776)

Scottish Homing Union: Mrs Gauld, Bank of Scotland Buildings, Hopetown Street, Bathgate, West Lothian, EH48 4EU (Bathgate 52943)

Welsh Homing Union: J.O. Davies, 26 Penybanc, Seven Sisters, Neath, Glamorgan (700498)

British Show Racer Federation: Secretary, Douglas Gifford, 29 Hope Close, Crossways, Dorchester, Dorset

National Pigeon Association: Secretary: E.H. Whitehead, Gerlan, Bryn Castell, Conwy, Gwynedd, LL32 8LF

National Tippler Union: Secretary, Brian Rose, 46 Maynard Road, Hartcliffe, Bristol, BS13 OAG

National Union of Short Distance Flyers: 53 Swithenbank Avenue, Ossett, Yorkshire, WF5 9RR

Appendix II
International Addresses

Fédération Colombophile Internationale: 39 Rue de Livourne, Ixelles 1050, Bruxelles, Belgium

Member Organisations

Argentina: Federaçion Colombofila Argentina, Corriente 5445–2° Piso of 7 Y 9, Buenos Aires

Australia: Pigeon Fanciers Protection Union of New South Wales, 24 Scott Street, Toongabbie West, 2146

Austria: Verband Österreichischer, Brieftaubenzuchtervereine, Deutschordenstrasse 20/1, 1140 Wien (94 19 875)

Belgium: Royale Fédération Colombophile Belge, 39 Rue de Livourne, Ixelles 1050, Bruxelles (537 6211)

Brazil: Associacao Brasilera de Colombophilia, Av Paranaiba, Centro (Estadio Olimpico), Caixa Postal No 840, 74,000 Goinia-Goinia-Goias

Bulgaria: Union Nationale Colombophile de Bulgarie, S. Srebarna, Silistrenkiokrag

Canada: Canadian Racing Pigeon Union Inc. Mrs Dorothy Joseph, RR No 4 London, Ontario, NGA 4B8 (519-681-1092)

China, Republic of: China Pigeon Racing Association, 4th Floor, 382 Min Chaun East Road, Taipai, Taiwan

Cuba: Federation Colombofila de Cuba, Escober No 104, Habana 2

Czechoslovakia: Ceskoslovensky Svaz, Chovatelu Drobneho Zvirectva, Maskova 3, Praha 8-Kobylisy 18253 (845742)

Denmark: De Danske Brevdueforeninger, Kirkevaerlosevej 24, 3500 Vaerloese

Egypt: Association Colombophile Egyptienne. Colonel Mohamed R. Abdel Fattah, 3 Amin El Shamsey Street, Cairo, Egypt

France: Union des Fédérations Régionales des Associations Colombophiles de France, 54 Boulevard Carnot, 59042 Lille Cedex (20 06 82 87)

Germany East: Sektion Sporttauben der DDR, 1071 Berlin, Wicherstrasse 10

Germany West: Verband Deutscher Brieftaubenliebhaber ev, 43 Essen, Postfach 1792, Schöneinstrasse 43

Great Britain: Royal Pigeon Racing Association (see Appendix I) North of England Homing Union (see Appendix I)

Holland: Nederlandse Postduivenhouders Organisatie. Secretary, H. Beumer, 10 Malistraat, Utrecht, Holland

Hungary: Maghar Postagalambsport Szovesteg, Verseny-U-16, Budapest, 1076 (424-522)

Italy: Federazione Colombofila Italiana, Piazza Zama 6, 00183 Roma

Japan: Japan Racing Pigeon Association, 17-11 Ueno Park, Daito-Ku, Tokyo 110

Korea: Address not available

Luxembourg: Fédération Colombophile Luxembourgeoise, Rue des Champs 16a, Bertrange

Malta: Federation of Pigeon Racing Clubs (Malta). Alfred Micallef, c/o De Naudi, Fleur de Lys Road, B'Kara, Malta

Mexico: Fédération Colombophile du Mexique. President, Mr Miguel Galeas Lavin, Portfiria Diaz 33, Mexico 12 DF

Norway: Norges Brevdueforbund v/Per-Kristian Hansen, Fuglevik Indre 3, 1600 Fredrikstad, Norway

Poland: Polski Zwiazek Hodowcow Golebi Pocztowynch, Zarzad Glowny, Katowice, UI Kosciuszki 68

Portugal: Federacao Portugesa de Columbofila, Rua Artur Paiva No 30, 1100 Lisboa, Portugal

Romania: Associatia Centrale a Crescatorilor de Porumbei, Strada Fagaras 14 (77108) Sector 6, Bucuresti (49 58 05)

South Africa: South African Homing Union, 102 Dr Euvrard Street, Malmesbury

Spain: Real Fedaracion Colombofila Espanola, c/Eloy Gonzalo 34, Piso 7°, Madrid 10 (448 8842)

Sweden: Svenska Brefduveforbunet, M. Tage Eriksson, Pl 4394 Bjarlov, 291 90 Kristianstad

Switzerland: Association Centrale des Sociétés Colombophiles. Mr Fre Zulauf, President, Murenbergstr. I, CH-4416 Bubendorf, Switzerland

Trinidad and Tobago: The National Racing Pigeon Association of Trinidad and Tobago, 3 Scott-Bushe, Port of Spain, Trinidad, West Indies

United States of America: The American Pigeon Racing Union. Charles E. Herin, Secretary-Treasurer, PO Box 26, Maineville, Ohio 45039

International Federation of American Homing Pigeon Fanciers Inc. Joe Rotondo, Secretary, 107 Jefferson Street, Belmont Hills, PA 19004 (215-667-0909)

Venezuela: Societad Colombofila de Venezuela, Avenida Santander, El Paraiso, Caracas

Yugoslavia: Savez Sportskuh Klubova, Uzgajivaca, Golobova Listonosa, 4100 Zagreb, Horvatovac 43

Further Reading

British Homing World published weekly
Racing Pigeon Pictorial published monthly
The Racing Pigeon published weekly

Feathered World Official journal of The National Pigeon Association and available only by subscription.

Barker, Dr W.E. *Pigeon Racing*, Racing Pigeon Publishing Co. 3 ed.

Barrett, G. *Racing Pigeons*, Cassell 1975.

McClary, D. *The Show Racer*, Faber & Faber 1976

Hall, F.W.S. *Pigeon Racing*, Racing Pigeon Publishing Co. 4 ed. 1975

Lovel, T. *Pierre Dordin*, Racing Pigeon Publishing 1984

Osman, Colin. *Racing Pigeons*, Faber & Faber 2 ed. 1980

Wheeler, H.G. *Exhibition and Flying Pigeons*, Spur Publications 1978

Index

Italic numerals denote illustrations

171